Suicide &
Self-Destructive Behaviors

YOUNG ADULT'S GUIDE TO THE SCIENCE OF HEALTH

Allergies & Asthma

Contraception & Pregnancy

Coping with Moods

Dental Care

Drug- & Alcohol-Related Health Issues

Fitness & Nutrition

Growth & Development

Health Implications of Cosmetic Surgery,
Makeovers, & Body Alterations

Healthy Skin

Managing Stress

Sexually Transmitted Infections

Sleep Deprivation & Its Consequences

Smoking-Related Health Issues

Suicide & Self-Destructive Behaviors

Weight Management

Young Adult's Guide to the Science of Health

Suicide &
Self-Destructive Behaviors

Joan Esherick

MASON CREST

Mason Crest
450 Parkway Drive, Suite D
Broomall, PA 19008
www.masoncrest.com

Printed in the Hashemite Kingdom of Jordan.

First printing
9 8 7 6 5 4 3 2 1

Series ISBN: 978-1-4222-2803-6
ISBN: 978-1-4222-2817-3
ebook ISBN: 978-1-4222-9013-2

The Library of Congress has cataloged the
        hardcopy format(s) as follows:

          Library of Congress Cataloging-in-Publication Data

Esherick, Joan.
  Suicide & self-destructive behaviors / Joan Esherick.
    pages cm. – (Young adult's guide to the science of health)
  Includes index.
  ISBN 978-1-4222-2817-3 (hardcover) – ISBN 978-1-4222-2803-6 (series) – ISBN 978-1-4222-9013-2 (ebook)
  1. Suicidal behavior–Juvenile literature. 2. Self-destructive behavior–Juvenile literature. 3. Self-destructive behavior in adolescence–Juvenile literature. 4. Teenagers–Suicidal behavior–Juvenile literature. 5. Youth–Suicidal behavior–Juvenile literature. I. Title. II. Title: Suicide and self-destructive behaviors.
  RC569.E84 2014
  616.85'8445–dc23
                          2013006393

Designed and produced by Vestal Creative Services.
www.vestalcreative.com

This book is meant to educate and should not be used as an alternative to appropriate medical care. Its creators have made every effort to ensure that the information presented is accurate and up to date—but this book is not intended to substitute for the help and services of trained medical professionals.

Contents

Introduction

by Dr. Sara Forman

You're not a little kid anymore. When you look in the mirror, you probably see a new person, someone who's taller, bigger, with a face that's starting to look more like an adult's than a child's. And the changes you're experiencing on the inside may be even more intense than the ones you see in the mirror. Your emotions are changing, your attitudes are changing, and even the way you think is changing. Your friends are probably more important to you than they used to be, and you no longer expect your parents to make all your decisions for you. You may be asking more questions and posing more challenges to the adults in your life. You might experiment with new identities—new ways of dressing, hairstyles, ways of talking—as you try to determine just who you really are. Your body is maturing sexually, giving you a whole new set of confusing and exciting feelings. Sorting out what is right and wrong for you may seem overwhelming.

Growth and development during adolescence is a multifaceted process involving every aspect of your being. It all happens so fast that it can be confusing and distressing. But this stage of your life is entirely normal. Every adult in your life made it through adolescence—and you will too.

But what exactly is adolescence? According to the American Heritage Dictionary, adolescence is "the period of physical and psychological development from the onset of puberty to adulthood." What does this really mean?

In essence, adolescence is the time in our lives when the needs of childhood give way to the responsibilities of adulthood. According to psychologist Erik Erikson, these years are a time of separation and individuation. In other words, you are separating from your parents, becoming an individual in your own right. These are the years when you begin to make decisions on your own. You are becoming more self-reliant and less dependent on family members.

When medical professionals look at what's happening physically—what they refer to as the biological model—they define the teen years as a period of hormonal transformation toward sexual maturity, as well as a time of peak growth, second only to the growth during the months of infancy. This physical transformation from childhood to adulthood takes place under the influence of society's norms and social pressures; at the same time your body is changing, the people around you are expecting new things from you. This is what makes adolescence such a unique and challenging time.

Being a teenager in North America today is exciting yet stressful. For those who work with teens, whether by parenting them, educating them, or providing services to them, adolescence can be challenging as well. Youth are struggling with many messages from society and the media about how they should behave and who they should be. "Am I normal?" and "How do I fit in?" are often questions with which teens wrestle. They are facing decisions about their health such as how to take care of their bodies, whether to use drugs and alcohol, or whether to have sex.

This series of books on adolescents' health issues provides teens, their parents, their teachers, and all those who work with them accurate information and the tools to keep them safe and healthy. The topics include information about:

- normal growth
- social pressures
- emotional issues
- specific diseases to which adolescents are prone
- stressors facing youth today
- sexuality

The series is a dynamic set of books, which can be shared by youth and the adults who care for them. By providing this information to educate in these areas, these books will help build a foundation for readers so they can begin to work on improving the health and well-being of youth today.

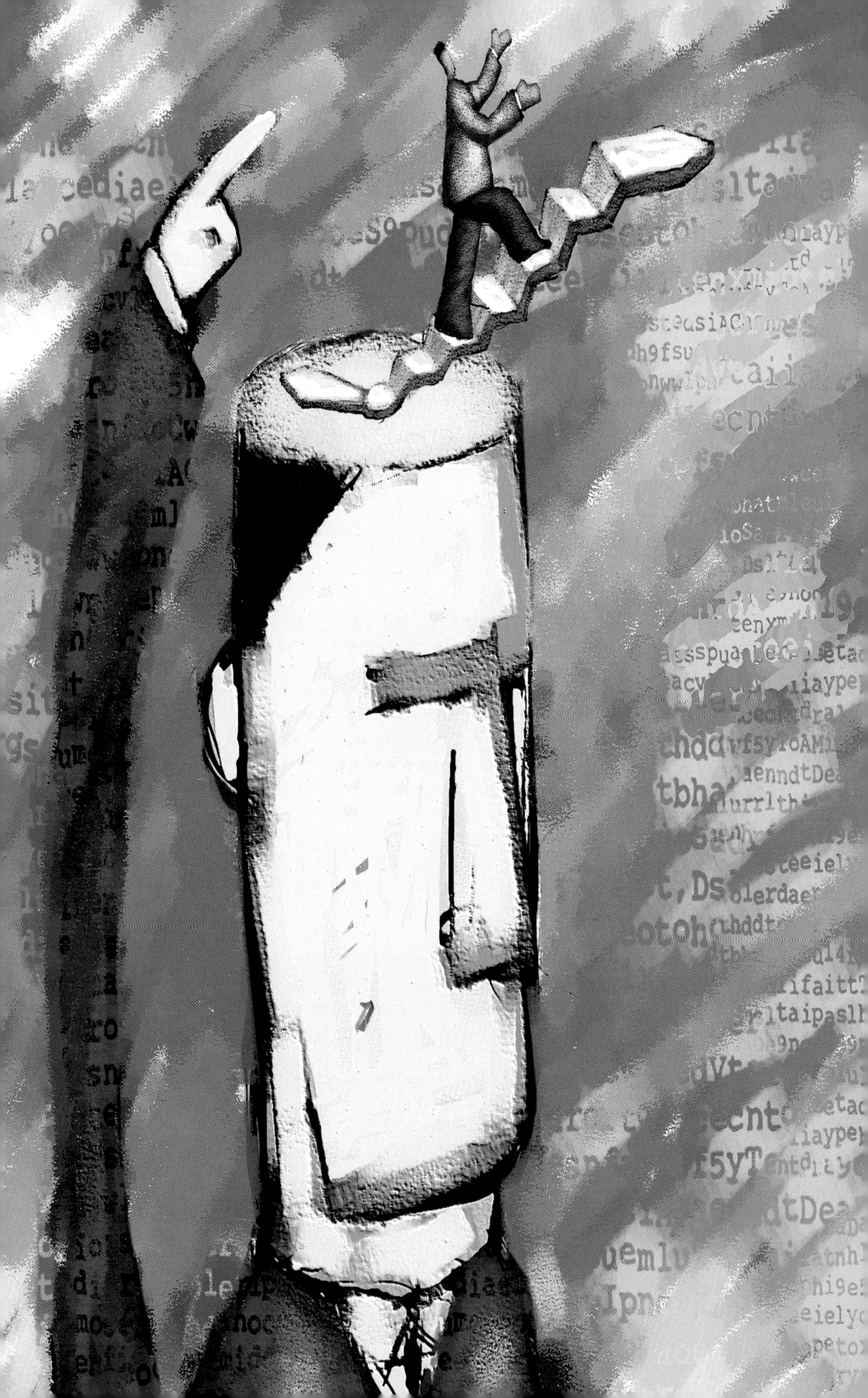

1

A Matter of Degree: Pushing the Limits Doesn't Have to Cause Harm

Sixteen-year-old Draven was pleased as he eyed himself in the candlelit mirror. The black bondage collar around his neck sharply contrasted with the pallor of his face. White foundation, black lipstick and eyeliner, thinly drawn arches in place of shaved eyebrows, and dyed jet-black hair all worked to create the living-dead look he wanted. His black leather pants, white poet's shirt with high open neck and ruffled cuffs, black leather vest, and silver ANKH hanging from the post in his ear shouted "Gothic nobility" to anyone who cared to notice.

Jamal could feel the sweat trickling beneath his helmet as he eyed the course in front of him. The middle banks gave him several options; he could GAP THE BANKS or play on the HITCHING POST from ROLL-INS on either side. The six-foot spine opposite the middle banks would make for great tailwhips and spins. The course's center, however, with its six-foot TABLETOP and four-foot super booter worried him. If he used the eight-foot quarter on the far side of the tabletop to gain speed, he might be able to launch off the super booter with enough lift to complete a full DOUBLE. If he made it, he'd score a personal best, maybe even place. If not, he might break something, but that would be nothing new. Broken bones were no stranger to this up-and-coming BMX stunt cyclist.

"No guts, no glory," the fifteen-year-old mumbled to himself as he launched his bike forward. Jamal would go for the double.

Kirsten tiptoed past her parents' dark bedroom, down the carpeted stairwell and into the dimly lit kitchen. The hood light above the stove glinted in the stainless steel blade as the young teen slid a serrated steak knife out of its maple knife block and into the pocket of her flannel robe. Her pounding heart and sweating palms gave the only evidence of her excitement as she crept back to the haven of her room. Relief couldn't come quickly enough.

The thirteen-year-old sat on the edge of her bed and turned the knife over in her hands. The building anticipation would provide an even greater release when she finally began. Inhaling sharply and holding her breath, Kirsten opened her robe, exposing her bare flesh, then pressed the knife's tip into her skin. Slowly, steadily she pushed the knifepoint until the first scarlet drops appeared. Knowing she'd broken through, she exhaled slowly, and then dragged the blade two inches across her thigh. A thin red line appeared. Lifting the knife and beginning again

Suicide & Self-Destructive Behaviors

in the same spot, she traced her first slice, cutting more deeply. Her blood flowed more fully this time.

Kirsten sighed. She felt the tightness in her neck begin to ease, as the bleeding relieved her anxiety. Her tension drained with her seeping blood. Cutting didn't hurt, really. Or if it did, she didn't feel it. All she felt was relief, the slow sweet release of her pent-up pain.

Lexi's relief came differently. Pulling out what was left of the nickel bag stuffed beneath her mattress, she opened the Ziploc, pinched a wad of weed between her fingertips, and sprinkled

Using cocaine is one form of risk-taking.

Suicide & Self-Destructive Behaviors

TOP FIVE KILLERS OF YOUNG PEOPLE AGED TWELVE TO NINETEEN IN 2006

1. Unintentional Injury: 48%
2. Homicide: 13%
3. Suicide: 11%
4. Malignant Neoplasms (Cancer): 6%
5. Heart Disease: 3%

the dried crumbled leaves across the center of the small paper square she held on her knees. Grasping the paper with the thumb and first two fingers of each hand, she carefully rolled the paper, licking the edge and ends of the paper tube she'd created to seal her treasure inside. She knew her parents might notice the pungent odor coming from her bedroom, even though she'd opened her windows, but she didn't care. It was worth the risk. Holding the joint to her lips, she lit up and inhaled. Anything to escape the awful anger she held inside.

Draven, Jamal, Kirsten, and Lexi—each of these teenagers sought avenues of self-expression; all were risk-takers in search of a thrill.

But they didn't all find relief by hurting themselves. One popular myth of adolescent risk-taking is that most teen behaviors and escape mechanisms are intentionally self-destructive. Not so, says FCD Educational Services of Newton, Massachusetts, a

comprehensive drug, alcohol, and tobacco-use prevention program implemented in public and private schools throughout the United States. In fact, most of the million-plus teens interviewed in this program stated that they started drinking, smoking, or doing drugs and other self-destructive behaviors not because they wanted to harm themselves, but "because they wanted to stop feeling bored, angry, hurt, worried, harassed, afraid, inadequate, OSTRACIZED, lonely, or anxious." They took risks not because they were self-destructive, but because they wanted to entertain themselves, find acceptance, or avoid difficult emotions.

Emotions run strong during the adolescent years, as does the need for acceptance. Risk-taking provides an outlet for runaway feelings and insecurities and provides a sure antidote to boredom, as the teens in the FCD programs affirmed. Risk-taking is also a part of normal teen growth and development. Teens are transitioning from dependence to independence, from childhood to adulthood, from their parents' ways to new beliefs and value systems. To become well-rounded, healthy, functioning adults, teens have to test the waters, explore the limits, and discover their individual places in the world.

Part of that exploration shows itself in testing known boundaries: staying out late, disobeying curfews, talking back to parents or teachers, skipping school, dressing like peers or rock stars, refusing to go to customary re-ligious services, changing eating habits, displaying extremes in emotion, slamming doors, arguing about little things, and refusing to do routine chores at home. Some teens push the boundaries further by engaging in behaviors that have the potential to cause harm.

The fact that youth engage in high-risk behaviors should be no surprise. But when does risk-taking go too far? When does it move from normal adolescent testing to dangerous self-destruction? What is the difference between healthy and unhealthy risk-taking? The answer, in part, is degree.

Healthy Risk-Taking Behaviors: Extreme Sports, Extreme Dress

Jamal's passion for BMX stunt biking made him take risks, even dangerous ones, but his desire wasn't self-destructive. He simply wanted to be the best he could be in his chosen sport, and that meant pushing the skill envelope beyond the limits of what he knew he could do. He followed his sport's safety guidelines (he wore a helmet, wrist guards, elbow and knee pads), but pursuing excellence came with risk, just as it does with any sport: football players break necks; soccer players tear ligaments; hockey players lose teeth; tennis players wreck elbows. If Jamal had to risk breaking his ankles or shattering his collarbone to attempt a double, then so be it. As far as he was concerned, it was an acceptable risk—just part of the sport. He didn't want to get hurt. But injury, he knew, was sometimes the cost of success.

TEN POPULAR EXTREME SPORTS

1. in-line skating
2. skateboarding
3. BMX stunt biking
4. snowboarding
5. surfing
6. rock climbing
7. adventure racing
8. street luging
9. bungee jumping
10. barefoot water- skiing

Participating in extreme sports like BMX stunt biking (as Jamal did), skateboarding, snowboarding, motocross racing, sky diving, bungee jumping, rock climbing, SPELUNKING, RAPPELLING, white-water rafting, downhill skiing, ski jumping, and other high-risk adventure sports comes with the possibility of injury. These are dangerous sports. But most teens who participate in them seek thrills, adventure, bragging rights, and acceptance; they aren't kids who want to hurt themselves.

The same could be said of adolescents like Draven, who use alternate clothing styles, body piercings, and tattoos as avenues for rebellion, belonging, and making philosophical statements, but who don't desire to do self-harm. Their risk-taking behaviors (including tattooing and piercing when done appropriately and safely) run only the risk of disapproval by parents or authorities and, perhaps, ostracism from their more conservative peers. Their counter-cultural ways are more statements of independent identity than attempts at self-destruction. As researchers concluded in a 2002 Brown University study on tattoos, piercing, and other adolescent risk-taking behaviors, "The presence of tattoos and body piercings in adolescents does not necessarily indicate risk-taking behavior in particular individuals." These teens may only desire to create an image of rebellion through appearance, not action, or they may be seeking admittance into a subculture of like-minded friends.

Extreme sports and alternate lifestyle expressions are only two of the risk-taking behaviors teens can undertake as part of a healthy testing-the-boundaries-process of growing up. What are other healthy avenues for pushing the limits?

1. Risking physical comfort. Test the limits of your body: Set a realistic fitness goal and pursue it. Try out for a sports team. If you're a runner or cyclist, increase your mileage; if you're a rock climber, increase the difficulty of your next

PIERCING AND TATTOOING SAFETY

Try these eight tips for safer tattooing and body piercing:

1. Do your research.
2. Go only to a professional, licensed practitioner.
3. Ask about sterilization procedures.
4. Ask about "universal precautions." The government has established these for handling blood and body fluids (largely to prevent the spread of hepatitis and HIV). If your salon doesn't ALWAYS follow these, don't go there.
5. Make an appointment only if someone can go with you.
6. When you arrive, if the salon looks dirty, the equipment looks used, or the practitioner looks unhealthy, walk out.
7. After the procedure, follow care instructions exactly until the wounds heal.
8. Call your doctor immediately if you show signs of infection.

climb. Sign up for a race or competition, or try an adventure camp.

2. Risking physical appearance. Try a new look, a new hairstyle, a new line of clothes. Wear a different kind of makeup or jewelry. Dress differently than you have before and see if the style suits you. If not, try another.

3. Risking intellectual confidence. Expand the limits of your mind. Sign up for a difficult class. Listen to a different genre of music. Set a reading goal and meet it. Learn a new skill. Try a new hobby. Write a letter to the editor of your local newspaper. Take a paramedic training course

HEALTHY RISK-TAKING BEHAVIORS

- experimenting with fashion or hair styles
- participating in team sports
- participating in extreme sports
- attending outdoor adventure camps
- starting a fitness regimen
- participating in a race or contest
- trying new hobbies or activities
- taking on new responsibilities (for example, starting a job)
- experimenting with new ways of thinking
- examining different faiths
- taking extracurricular classes
- listening to different music styles
- going somewhere you've never been before
- making a new friend
- participating in community service
- participating in school or local government
- becoming involved in social protest or philosophical debate

or learn CPR. Enroll in a college course while you're still in high school.

4. Risking emotional security. Push the limits of your feelings. Are you afraid of roller coasters? Make yourself ride one. Are you too intimidated to ask someone out on a date? Give that person a call. Do you dread speaking in public? Run for school government or public office. Step outside your comfort zone, perhaps by tackling a com-

Suicide & Self-Destructive Behaviors

munity service project or volunteering for a committee. Face your fears, and try a new challenge.

5. Risking spiritual complacency. Explore the limits of your spiritual health. Get more involved in your church, temple, mosque, or synagogue. Study your faith and the faiths of others. Interview someone of a different faith. Go on a mission trip. Take a spiritual pilgrimage. Help in a homeless shelter, or volunteer to deliver food to the poor. Think of a small way you can change the world for the better; then develop a plan and implement it.

These are healthy risks adolescents can take to make statements about their identities and independence without compromising their health or safety. Not all teens, however, are content with these risks. Some teens would rather indulge in behaviors so dangerous they threaten their health, long-term well-being, and even their lives.

High-Risk Behaviors in Teens—Unintentional Harm

The 2006 Youth Risk Behavior Surveillance study done by the U.S. Centers for Disease Control (CDC) found that high-risk behaviors accounted for nearly 48 percent of all deaths of young people between the ages of twelve and nineteen. The CDC identified the top three teenage killers as unintentional injury, homicide, and suicide, which accounted for 72 percent of the young people who died in the United States in that year.

High-risk behaviors don't always end in death; sometimes they leave the person scarred, sick, or permanently disabled. Teens like Kirsten, who self-injure, may find themselves addicted to cutting after only one episode and facing a future of shame, scars, relapses, and recoveries. Adolescents like Lexi, our

In 2009, unintentional injuries were the cause of 9,000 deaths; 225,000 hospitalizations; and 8.4 million emergency room treatments. Unintentional injuries are the number-one cause of death among teens.

drug user, may ride a downward spiral of increasingly more dangerous addictions: first marijuana, then ecstasy, then cocaine or heroin. Shared needles may one day leave her with HEPATITIS or HIV, while drug-induced sexual encounters may leave her ravaged by sexually transmitted infections (STIs) or unable to have children.

Self-injury and substance abuse, while serious, aren't the only self-destructive behaviors considered high risk by the CDC. The leading cause of adolescent death by far is unintentional injury; and the leading cause of unintentional injury is motor vehicle accidents (MVAs). According to the National Center for Injury Prevention and Control, the risk for MVAs is higher among sixteen- to nineteen-year-olds than any other age group. In 2010, 2,700 teens died from motor vehicle accidents, which means that seven teens died per day. Teens are three times more likely, mile-for-mile, to be involved in a crash than older drivers.

Why do teens account for so high a percentage of MVAs? It isn't just inexperience with driving, though this accounts for part of the statistic, nor is it just the well-known cost of driving sleepy, drunk, or high, though these, too, take a heavy toll on adolescent lives. Participation in the following risky behaviors can also result in MVA injuries and deaths: driving at excessive speeds, running red lights, not wearing seat belts, riding with someone who has been drinking or using drugs, ignoring weather or road conditions, ignoring traffic hazards, having

Suicide & Self-Destructive Behaviors

sexual contact while driving, being distracted while driving (using cell phones, CD players, etc.), or drag racing.

Automobile accidents, however, are only one of several causes of unintentional injury. According to the same CDC study, though motor vehicle accidents accounted for the largest number of unintentional deaths in teens, poisoning, drowning, other land transport accidents (motorcycles, ATVs, etc.), firearms, burns, bikes, and suffocation kill or injure thousands of adolescents each year.

Almost daily, with little thought to the risks, teens all over America refuse to wear seat belts, handle guns carelessly, drive too fast, and ride helmetless on bikes, motorcycles, and ATVs. These behaviors, like body piercing and BMX bike riding, are usually done without the intention to do self-harm. They are all just part of typical teenage thrill seeking and limit testing.

FIVE STEPS TO REDUCING YOUR RISK OF INJURY OR DEATH

1. Always wear a seat belt when in a car (driving or riding).
2. Stay away from guns and gangs.
3. Wear a helmet when on skateboards, in-line skates, bikes, and motorized vehicles.
4. Don't drive drunk or high. Don't ride with someone who is drunk or high.
5. Don't swim or dive while drunk or high.

UNHEALTHY RISK-TAKING BEHAVIORS

- trying tobacco (cigarettes, cigars, pipes, smokeless tobacco)
- drinking alcohol
- huffing (doing inhalants)
- experimenting with other drugs
- driving under the influence (or riding with someone who is)
- driving at excessive speeds (or riding with someone who is)
- fasting, restricting food intake, or bingeing and purging
- participating in dangerous sports without appropriate protective or safety gear
- using weapons or firearms
- engaging in casual or high-risk sexual activity
- viewing or participating in pornography
- gambling or betting on sports
- partying with strangers
- joining a cult or gang
- running away from home
- stealing or shoplifting
- committing violent acts (for example, bullying, assault, rape, or molestation)
- self-mutilating (cutting, pursuing excessive piercings, tattoos, and cosmetic surgeries)

Suicide & Self-Destructive Behaviors

Combining alcohol and driving is an unhealthy risk-taking behavior.

Complicating this thrill-seeking lust for adventure is the belief held by most teenagers that nothing bad can ever happen to them. They see themselves as invincible. When experiences (or statistics) prove otherwise, as they often do, many teen behaviors can be easily addressed: keep guns under lock and key; wear seat belts whenever getting into a car, put on a helmet when using bikes or motorcycles; and obey the speed limit. These safer behaviors replace higher-risk ones when teens find the motivation to change.

Some behaviors, however, are more complicated and much harder to change.

Self-Destructive Behaviors in Teens: A Silent Cry

Consider these statistics. Over the next twenty-four hours in the United States:

- Fourteen young people between the ages of fifteen and twenty-four will successfully commit suicide (Safe School Helpline).
- Another 1,400 teens will attempt suicide.
- Over 2,000 teen girls between the ages of fifteen and nineteen will become pregnant (stayteen.org).
- Over 10,000 teens will contract a sexually transmitted infection (National Institutes of Health).
- Nearly 4,000 kids will try their first cigarette (Campaign for Tobacco-Free Kids).
- Another 1,000 will become daily smokers (HHS, SAMHSA).
- Over 15,000 teens will try drugs for the first time (truth-talks.org).
- In the next year, one of every hundred adolescent girls will develop an eating disorder (Center of Excellence in Eating Disorders).

- Between 14 to 17 percent have self-injured by the time they are 18 (ASCD).

These high-risk issues will be addressed in the next several chapters. While there are not any quick cures for these disorders, many teens do recover with psychiatric help. Substance abuse, casual sex, cutting, eating disorders, and suicidal thoughts and behaviors are self-destructive, life-threatening responses to teen ANGST that can be helped if taken seriously. If ignored and left untreated, all can lead to death or lifelong health issues for those involved.

Unlike Draven and Jamal, two of the teens discussed earlier in this chapter, teens who practice these high-risk activities aren't

YOUTH VIOLENCE— MORE RISKY BEHAVIORS

For teenagers between the ages of fifteen and nineteen, homicide is the second leading cause of death, second only to unintentional injury. Up to 84 percent of youth homicides involve firearms, while 8 percent involve cutting or stabbing.

Youth violence can take other forms: rape, sexual assault, robbery, bullying. The rates of nonfatal victimization are higher among people under age twenty-five than any other age group. One in six high school students surveyed (grades nine through twelve) admitted to carrying weapons within the last thirty days, and around 11 percent reported being involved in a physical fight at least once in the previous year.

Try to stay away from unhealthy activities and make good decisions!

Suicide & Self-Destructive Behaviors

TELLING THE DIFFERENCE

How do you distinguish unhealthy risk-taking from healthy risk-taking? Ask yourself these questions:

- Can this activity adversely affect my health, safety, or well-being?
- Can this activity hurt me or other people?
- Can this activity make me or others sick?
- Will this activity open the door to other health or safety risks?
- Is this activity illegal?
- Am I ashamed of this activity?
- Can this activity kill someone?

If you answered "yes" to any of the above questions, the activity is an unhealthy risk. If you are compelled to take unhealthy risks, seek help—it's not necessary to risk losing your life or health.

simply seeking thrills, making statements, rebelling against norms, or looking for acceptance. These teens are writhing in silent pain, screaming silent screams, and crying silent cries for help.

2

CHEMICAL ENHANCEMENT:
Substance Abuse
from Rehab to Rave

Case One

I started using drugs when I was only twelve. I was hanging out with a lot of older kids and they were doing them so I figured if they were doing drugs and seemed fine, then I could do them and still be fine. It started with only smoking pot every weekend to, in a matter of weeks, drinking and taking E (ecstasy) every night. I needed a drink or a smoke every couple of hours. I was sick some nights when I couldn't get my hands on anything. Being only twelve, I couldn't get money to support my habit. My so-called "friend" told me how to get money. He said that if I slept with him, he would give me $100. Back then, I thought that was a lot of money, but looking back on it now, that was one of the worst mistakes of my life. I started sleeping with guys just to get some pot or E. By the time I was thirteen, my grades had slipped, I lost most of my friends, and I was depressed. I had lost four friends to overdoses, suicide, and drunk drivers, one of whom was my boyfriend at the time. One night after my parents found out that I had been dating a nineteen-year-old, I tried to kill myself. After that I realized I had a problem and needed to get help. I also realized that the people that I hung out with were not my true "friends." They were just using me to get what they wanted and wouldn't be there to help me when I needed them. Now I am almost fourteen and have been clean for about six months. I guess it all happened for one reason: so I could appreciate how good life can be if I make the right choices.

Case Two

As a sixteen-year-old high school student, everywhere I turn I hear about drugs. My town is very small and everyone knows each other. One night a few of my friends went to a rave where there were a lot of drugs. One of my friends got high on weed first, and then someone talked him into doing ecstasy. Soon after he took it, he started doing all kinds of crazy things: hallucinating, cursing people out, blacking out. The worst part was when he started having a seizure! After that, he blacked out and never came back. They rushed him to the area hospital, but doctors couldn't help him. Today I still think about my friend. I miss him so much.

Case Three

I had a horrible experience on the drug ecstasy. I had taken it a couple times before, and it was enjoyable. The last time I tried it, I started with only a half of a tablet. My friends and I were watching TV and gossiping about everybody when it hit me. It only took about three minutes, which is very unusual. All the blood rushed from my head to my feet. I thought I was going to collapse. I had to move around. It was only thirty-five degrees outside but I had to run up and down the block or I thought I'd go crazy. Those effects lasted about thirty minutes. We went to a club an hour later, and I was just feeling relaxed and mellow when all of a sudden I felt like laughing gas had been pumped into the room. My head felt light, and I couldn't think straight. It was kind of cool for a while, but those effects lasted for THREE DAYS!!!! I couldn't shake it. I couldn't drive. I was scared to go to the store. I couldn't function. I will never do it again.

Case Four

I went to a party with some people I just met. I was with three other people, and I've never had a safety issue before. Besides, I'm sixteen and bulletproof. We were all drinking, and my best friend was with me, and apparently someone slipped something into her drink. I'm not sure what, but these boys kept throwing around words like GHB and roofies. I had to slap my friend to wake her, but even then it didn't enter my head that she was drugged. I put her pants on her while she struggled and grunted, telling me, "No, no, no." I kept telling her it was okay, it was time to go. I thought she had too much to drink. I'd seen her pretty wasted in the past, and this didn't seem much different. But I've never had to clothe her or get physical in any way, shape, or form to get her to move. I pulled her off the bed several times while her head bobbed around as if she had no muscles in her neck. She opened her eyes once in a while and said, "Okay." But mostly she was incoherent and babbling. She threw up. A lot. I'd just like to know what happened. There was no way two shots

could have done that to her. There was no way a beer could make her have this much of a hangover. The guys were talking about date-rape drugs, and I think they gave her some. I hate looking back and feeling stupid.

Case Five

I was at my friend's house kicking back, and she asked if I wanted to go to a party. I said yes, so we went. We were just chilling—drinking and smoking pot. I don't know how much I drank, but I just started taking shots and smoking blunts with these four guys. When I woke up, I was lying in the bed with my clothes off and the two guys were lying beside me. I never wanted to lose my virginity that way. I never wanted to lose my virginity at age fourteen.

The accounts you've just read are the words of real teens describing real experiences. Adapted from their anonymous posts on the Partnership for Drug Free America's website, www.drug-free.org, their stories reveal the hard, sometimes ugly truth about substance abuse.

What can we learn from them? Let's look at what these teens have in common.

Why People Start Taking Drugs

In all the accounts, the narrators started smoking, drinking, or using drugs because they were invited to do so. Most people start this way. A "friend" or older person offers drugs, the teens are curious, they want to be accepted or approved of, or they want to look "cool" or "grown-up," so they agree. The common assumption new users make is, If it's not hurting them, then it won't hurt me. Another assumption is, If I try it just this once,

Using chemicals to enhance your mood may have dangerous consequences.

nothing can happen; one time can't hurt. Both assumptions are wrong.

Huffing (sniffing common household products' fumes) and using common "club drugs" can result in addiction and/or death the very first time they are tried. In Case Two above, when the narrator's friend first used ecstasy, taking just one dose, he experienced seizures and other complications that killed him. His story isn't uncommon. According to an article from WebMD Drug News, complications from ecstasy caused nearly 17,865 emergency room visits in the United States in 2008.

Even alcohol, when used only once and combined with driving, can be fatal. According to the National Highway Traffic Safety Administration, an alcohol-related motor vehicle accident kills someone every fifty-three minutes and injures another person every ninety seconds. Twenty-five percent of these deaths involve fifteen to twenty-year-olds. Sometimes it's not the drug itself that kills; it's the action a person takes while under the influence that harms him.

When Frank Smith, a motivational speaker who has shared his story with more than 47,000 young people across North America, was twenty-two years old, he went out to party with some friends after having a fight with his girlfriend. He got drunk, then got high on crank (speed, meth), and climbed a tree. The next thing he remembers is waking up from a coma eight weeks later only to realize he would never walk again. A forty-foot fall from the tree he climbed while high put him in a wheelchair for life. His story illustrates how one stupid action while high or drunk can change a person's life forever.

Another assumption made by first-time drug users is, I can handle it. This, too, is a delusion. Look again at Cases One and Five. In both cases, the students involved lost control of their abilities to think straight and make rational decisions, and in one case, lost consciousness. Both suffered unwanted sexual

Suicide & Self-Destructive Behaviors

consequences as a result: one turned to prostitution to support her almost immediate addiction; the other was either raped or gave consent while impaired (because she can't remember, she'll never know). Neither woke up one morning and decided this was what she wanted for her life. Each thought she could handle the substances she chose to take, and ended up with unwanted experiences.

Ignorance of the danger, the desire to be liked or accepted, the longing to grow up fast, the need for approval, anger, the desire to rebel, the need for escape from a troubled home life

WHY PEOPLE TRY DRUGS

- curiosity
- boredom
- pressure from friends
- the promise of good feelings or stress reduction
- the desire to be liked or accepted
- the desire to look "cool" or mature
- the desire to escape difficult emotions
- thrill or adventure seeking
- anger
- insecurity
- ignorance of the dangers
- denial of the dangers
- immaturity
- lack of preparedness
- low self-worth
- low self-confidence
- unhealthy home environment

WHY SOME PEOPLE BECOME ADDICTED TO DRUGS

- The drug they try first is addictive.
- It feels good and momentarily reduces stress.
- They need more of the same drug to produce the same effects after using it for a while.
- They develop a tolerance (which means they don't get the same effect from the same amount of the drug. Therefore, they need to use something stronger to achieve that same feeling.)
- Their first drug lowers their inhibitions, opening the door to harder, more addictive drugs. People make bad decisions when they are under the influence of drugs. It is not unusual to hear a teenager say that they were drunk when they first tried drugs.
- Their social lives (friends, hangouts, etc.) become centered around drug use, which results in them losing their good friends who don't engage in these behaviors.
- They have a biological predisposition to addiction.
- They have other psychological disorders that make them prone to addiction.
- They grow up in a drug-using family or environment.
- They use drugs as a coping mechanism for handling painful emotions.

Teens may underestimate the effect that alcohol has on their reflexes when driving.

or emotional pain—all these can contribute to a person's decision to start drinking or doing drugs. Yet in every case a conscious decision is made to participate; each teen makes a choice, though sometimes misinformed. Even in Case Four, where one young woman is slipped a date-rape drug, both women made the choice to put themselves at risk by voluntarily choosing to attend the party and voluntarily choosing to drink.

In order to make the best choices, young people need to be well informed. Let's look at the facts then. After weighing them, you decide if substance abuse is worth the risk.

Facts About Specific Drugs

Though it would be impossible to discuss every potentially abused drug in this chapter, the following (summarized from information provided by the National Institute on Drug Abuse) will give you some valuable information so you know the facts about commonly abused drug substances before you try them. For additional information, consult other books in this series entitled *Drug and Alcohol-Related Health Issues* and *Smoking-Related Health Issues*.

Tobacco Products

DRUG NAME: nicotine
STREET NAME(S): cigarettes, cigars, smokeless tobacco, chew, snuff
DRUG FORM: rolled, wadded, caked
HOW TAKEN: smoked, snorted, wadded in mouth, spit
EFFECTS: increases heart rate and blood pressure, gives feelings of energy, increases mental alertness, reduces appetite, can cause weight loss

HEALTH HAZARDS: rapid addiction, can cause CHRONIC lung disease, heart disease, stroke, mouth and throat cancers, other cancers, pregnancy complications, skin damage, and is a gateway to other drugs

Pot and Other Hemp Products

DRUG NAME: marijuana or hashish

STREET NAMES: for marijuana—dope, grass, pot, herb, joints, Mary Jane, reefer, ganja, skunk, weed, blunt, sinsemilla; for hashish—boom, chronic, gangster, hash, hash brownie, hash oil, hemp, Juicy Fruit, Northern Lights, Bubble Gum

DRUG FORM: dried leaves rolled in paper smoked as cigarettes, smoked in pipes or bongs, smoked in hollowed-out cigars called "blunts," mixed into foods, or brewed as tea

HOW TAKEN: usually smoked, swallowed in food or tea

EFFECTS: slows thinking, slows reaction time, gives feelings of euphoria, causes confusion, impaired balance and coordination, and paranoia

HEALTH HAZARDS: addictive, causes frequent respiratory infections, chronic cough, PANIC ATTACKS, need for increased usage for same effect, impaired memory, learning difficulties, increased heart rate, anxiety, and is a gateway to harder drugs

Inhalants

DRUG NAME: inhalants

STREET NAMES: Amys, bang, bolt, head cleaner, huff, kick, pearls, poor man's pot, rush, moon gas, snappers, whippets

DRUG FORM: chemicals found in common household products: aerosols (spray paint, deodorant, hair spray, etc.); solvents (paint

WHAT'S A RAVE?

Rave:
a high-energy, all-night dance party held at a club or temporary venue (abandoned warehouses, open fields, empty buildings). Club drugs are commonly used at raves.

Rave music:
fast, pounding techno, trance, drum 'n bass music with choreographed laser-light programs.

Rave dress:
comfortable, lightweight, loose-fitting clothes worn in layers: T-shirts, tank tops, tube tops, open-back halter tops, bikini tops, loose-fitting shorts, or baggy pants. For themed raves, people come dressed according to theme (cartoon characters, gothic costumes, mystic dress, etc.).

Rave accessories:
glow-in-the-dark necklaces, bright colored beads or bracelets, glow sticks, baby pacifiers and lollipops (to offset teeth grinding caused by some club drugs), painter's masks caked with menthol vapor rub, flashing light pins of various shapes and sizes.

thinner, correction fluid, lighter fluid, felt-tip markers, nail polish, nail polish remover); adhesives (rubber cement, model airplane glue, other glues), gases (nitrous oxide, ether, chloroform); cleaning agents (dry-cleaning fluid, spot remover, degreasers); food products (whipped cream aerosols, cooking spray)
HOW TAKEN: "huffed," inhaled from soaked rags, containers, or

Teens may buy an illegal substance to enhance a "good time," but the chemical may have physical and emotional effects that are ultimately destructive.

substance-filled bags, sniffed from shirt cuffs or sleeves, inhaled from balloons.

EFFECTS: causes a quick, short-lasting high, stimulating effects, reduced INHIBITIONS, headaches, nausea, slurred speech, and loss of motor coordination

HEALTH HAZARDS: can be immediately addicting, can cause unconsciousness, muscle cramping, and memory impairment, damages the CARDIOVASCULAR SYSTEM, damages the nervous system, and can cause sudden death

Cough and Cold Products

DRUG NAME: DXM (dextromethorphan)

STREET NAMES: dex, DM, robo, rojo, skittles, triple C, velvet

DRUG FORM: nonprescription over-the-counter cough and cold medicines, liquids, tablets, lozenges, tablets, capsules, gel caps, and (less so) DXM powder

HOW TAKEN: swallowed (liquid, capsules, or pills), inhaled, or snorted (powder)

EFFECTS: causes a long-lasting high, hallucinations, dissociation (feeling removed from reality), visual distortions, nausea, vomiting, headache, tingling/numbness in hands and feet

HEALTH HAZARDS: irregular heartbeat, dehydration (from vomiting), loss of consciousness, seizures, brain damage, and sudden death

Ecstasy

DRUG NAME: MDMA (methylenedioxymethamphetamine)

STREET NAME: ecstasy, E, Adam, Eve, XTC, X, STP, peace, essence, hug drug, B-bombs, clarity, love drug, scooby snacks, sweeties, speed for lovers

DRUG FORM: tablets (various colors) imprinted with smiley faces, clover leaves, cartoon characters, or commercial brand logos (Nike, Mercedes, etc.)

EFFECTS: causes a slow-acting high, mild hallucinations, increased TACTILE sensation, increased feelings of love, compassion, empathy, feelings of exhilaration, increased mental alertness, rapid heart or irregular heartbeat, reduced heart rate, weight loss, nervousness, confusion, inability to sleep, involuntary teeth clenching, blurred vision, chills, sweating, paranoia

HEALTH HAZARDS: can be immediately addicting, can cause depression, insomnia, impaired memory, impaired learning abilities, exceptionally high fever, CARDIAC damage, liver damage, kidney failure, overdose death, and irreparable damage to cells in the brain.

Prescription Drugs

DRUG NAMES: various, but the most commonly abused are prescribed steroids, prescribed drugs containing codeine, Ritalin, and Ketamine (a veterinary anesthetic)

STREET NAMES:

- steroids—Arnolds, gym candy, juice, pumpers, stackers, weight trainers
- drugs with codeine—Empirin with Codeine, Fiorinal with Codeine, Robitussin A-C, Tylenol with Codeine, Captain Cody, Cody, schoolboy, doors & fours, loads, pancakes and syrup
- Ritalin—Kibbles and bits, kiddy cocaine, pineapple, Skippy, Smarties, vitamin R, west coast
- Ketamine—K, Special K, cat valium, vitamin K, green K, honey oil, jet, ket, Kit-Kat, purple, super acid, super C

DRUG FORM:

- steroids—tablet, liquid, gel, and cream
- drugs with codeine—liquid or tablet
- Ritalin—white or yellow tablets, sometimes crushed to produce powder or dissolved in water to produce liquid
- Ketamine—colorless, odorless liquid or white or off-white powder

HOW TAKEN:

- steroids—injected, swallowed, or applied to skin
- drugs with codeine—injected or swallowed
- Ritalin—swallowed, snorted, or injected
- Ketamine—mixed in beverages, added to other smokable drugs and smoked, snorted, swallowed, or injected

EFFECTS:

- steroids—no intoxicating effects; used to increase muscle strength
- drugs with codeine—pain relief, euphoria, drowsiness, SEDATION
- Ritalin—wakefulness, euphoria, increased focus, increased ability to concentrate
- Ketamine—distorted perceptions of sight and sound, feelings of disconnectedness, hallucinations, sensory impairment, amnesia, impaired coordination

HEALTH HAZARDS:

- steroids—addictive, can cause liver and kidney tumors, cancer, JAUNDICE, high blood pressure, severe acne, infertility, reduced sperm count, baldness, dramatic mood swings, "roid rage," depression, paranoid jealousy, extreme irritability, delusions, risk of needle-born diseases (HIV, hepatitis B and C, etc.)
- drugs with codeine—highly addictive with increased need for more to get same effect, can cause constipation, confusion, sedation, respiratory depression and arrest, unconsciousness, coma, and death
- Ritalin—can cause PSYCHOTIC episodes, facial TICS, cardiovascular complications, severe psychological addiction, small blood-vessel blockage, risk of needle-borne diseases (HIV, hepatitis B and C, etc.)
- Ketamine—can cause depression, delirium, amnesia, impaired motor function, potentially fatal respiratory problems, partial or complete incapacitation (which puts the user at additional risk of sexual assault)

These are just a few of the hundreds of substances abused in North America each day. Most of these are considered "gateway" drugs: that is, they are the first drugs new users are exposed to.

Gateway drugs can open the door to much harder drugs, including cocaine, crack cocaine, heroin, LSD, methamphetamines, and barbiturates. Gateway drugs are more commonly used among teenagers. They frequently are the stepping-stones to more dangerous, addictive drug use even for adolescents. The common factor that each of these drugs has is its potential to destroy or end lives.

HOW MANY TEENS REALLY DO USE DRUGS?

If you're considering using drugs because "everyone else is doing it," think again:

According to the 2010 National Household Survey on Drug Abuse (NHSDA), 3 percent reported prescription drug abuse in the last month—but nearly 97 percent did not. The 2011 Monitoring the Future survey reported that the overall substance dependence or abuse rate for twelve- to seventeen-year-olds was 7.4 percent, or less than one in ten teens.

The 2011 Monitoring the Future survey also described current cigarette smoking rates: "18.7 percent of 12th-graders reported current (past-month) cigarette use, compared to a recent peak rate of 36.5 percent in 1997 and 21.6 [in 2006]. Only 6.1 percent of eighth-graders reported current smoking, compared to a recent peak of 21 percent in 1996 and 8.7 percent [in 2006]."

According to the National Institute on Drug Abuse (NIDA), less than two percent of high school students use club drugs regularly. Ninety-eight percent do not. Ninety-four percent of teens have never tried Ecstasy.

(NIDA's Monitoring the Future study)

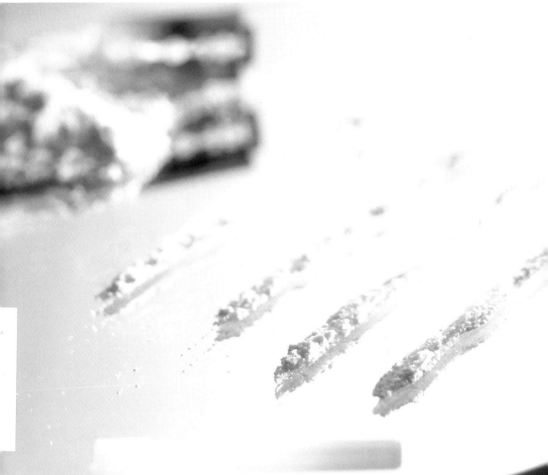

Teens who experiment with "gateway" drugs may eventually try more dangerous drugs, like cocaine.

The Cost

The case studies in this chapter reveal some of the serious risks of drug use. Many teens believe that the "mild" drugs are not dangerous. There is no such thing as a "mild" drug. Virtually all drug use can result in addiction, which leads to tragedy: lost

HOW DO I KNOW IF I HAVE A PROBLEM?

According to the American Psychiatric Association's Diagnostic and Statistical Manual, volume IV, you are probably addicted to a substance if any three or more of the following occur at any time in the same twelve-month period:

- You take the substance in larger amounts or over longer periods than intended.
- You experience persistent desire or unsuccessful effort to cut down on or control use of the substance.
- You spend a lot of time trying to acquire the substance, using the substance, or recovering from its effects.
- You stop doing things that were once important to you because of your substance usage (sports, homework, job, activities, hanging out with non-using friends, etc.).
- You keep taking the substance even though it makes you physically, emotionally, or psychologically sick.
- You need more of the substance to get the desired effects.
- You experience withdrawal if you try to stop taking the substance.

friendships, lost family relationships, lost self-esteem, lost reputations, dropping grades, lost innocence, victimization, rape, unsafe sex, addiction, lost jobs, financial trouble, lost trust, lost health, lost futures, lost dreams, and lost lives. The important questions that you need to ask yourself before you experiment with drugs are: is the thrill of getting high for one night or the need to satisfy a curiosity really worth the risk of getting addicted and losing everything that you have worked so hard for? You are the only one that can make that decision. Remember, it's your choice.

3

Risky Relationships:
Casual Sex in a World of STIs

I never thought it could happen to me, Amy wrote in her flower-covered journal. It was the one place she knew she could be honest. It was the only place she could be real. How could she ever tell anyone? At least she could confide in her silent, paper friend.

It was my first time, ever, she continued in her loopy, long-hand script. *Kev was the one; I just knew he was the one. He told me he'd never been with a girl. He told me we could wait; we didn't have to*

Regular school attendance reduces adolescent sexual risk-taking behavior. In the United States, teens who drop out of school are more likely to start sexual activity at younger ages, to not use contraception, to become pregnant, and to give birth.

(Surgeon General's Call to Action to Promote Sexual Health and Responsible Sexual Behavior, 2001)

go all the way. He told me he'd be patient. He didn't want to force me. But I loved him, and I wanted to show him I loved him. And I thought he loved me. He said he did. He treated me like he did—you know, like he gave me things, presents, flowers, stuff. He said we'd get married as soon as we were out of school. As soon as we both turned eighteen and didn't need our parents' approval. So we did it. We did the big IT. I gave him my heart, my soul, my body, my virginity. I gave him my love. I gave everything I had to give. And you know what he gave me? Herpes—a stupid STI that he must have gotten from someone else. That and a quick "so long, sucker." We had sex, then boom—he was outta here. He used me. That's all he ever really wanted. How could I be so dumb? What am I going to do now?

I don't care what they say, Janelle thought as she stormed out of her parents' house, slamming the door behind her. *I don't care if they don't want me to go to the club. Everyone else is going, and Tory will be there. I'm going, and they can't stop me.*

Seventeen-year-old Janelle, or "J" as her friends called her, jumped into her Geo Metro and sped off into the night. She arrived at Club Rave in less than ten minutes. There must have been two hundred people there already, and the all-night party had just begun.

THE LINK BETWEEN CHILDHOOD SEXUAL ABUSE AND TEEN PROMISCUITY

According to a report in the *American Journal of Public Health*, a study done by University of Albany's School of Criminal Justice found a direct relationship between childhood sexual abuse and teen prostitution. The report indicated that early childhood abuse and/or neglect was a significant predictor of prostitution. Females who were sexually abused were three times more likely to end up in teenage prostitution than those not abused.

Donning her glow-in-the-dark neck ring and bright beaded bracelets, she paid the cover charge and made her way into the pulsing crowd. Everyone seemed so happy, so at peace with themselves and the world. Everyone else seemed like they belonged. Everyone, that is, except her.

Where is Tory? she wondered as she scanned the gyrating teens in front of her. Strobe lights and lasers flashed in her eyes as she searched for her new friend.

"Yo, J, you made it." Tory came up to her from behind. "I was wondering when you'd get here. You want something to drink?"

Janelle turned toward his voice. "Yeah sure, got anything diet?" She tried to act cool, even nonchalant.

"Back in a flash."

Janelle watched her friend disappear into the crowd and then return with two red plastic cups of bubbling soda. He handed her one, then sipped his own.

"Hey, this isn't just soda!" Janelle objected after taking a sip.

"Ahh, lighten up." Tory winked at her and grinned. "It's just rum and Coke. It won't hurt you … it will help you relax."

"You sure?"

"Cross my heart." Tory gave Janelle his best you-can-trust-me-I'm-as-harmless-as-a puppy-dog look, and the matter was settled. She took another sip.

It's just booze. No big deal, Janelle remembers thinking. In about thirty minutes she realized it wasn't just booze. Her blurred vision warned her that something else was going on. Then she started to feel light-headed and weak, but could do nothing to help herself. The next thing she knew she was in a secluded back room with Tory on top of her. Then she passed out completely.

"Sure, baby, whatever you want." Dani sighed as she snuggled up next to Nick on the backseat of his car. "What will it be?" she whispered, trying to sound seductive.

"Everything." Nick sneered as he moved over her.

She could smell his sweat mixed with booze. She felt the roughness of his unshaven face graze her neck. He felt heavy as he pressed against her.

Dani opened her eyes as he buried his face in her chest and stared past him at the night sky, almost as if she were looking for heaven.

Another night. Another guy. Maybe Daddy was right all those years ago, the teenager thought for the hundredth time. Then, as if praying, she silently asked whoever or whatever was there, Is this all I'm worth? Is this really what You made me for?

WHICH TEENS ARE AT GREATEST RISK FOR HIGH-RISK SEXUAL BEHAVIORS?

- Teens who drink or do drugs
- Teens who have been physically or sexually abused
- Teens for whom religion or spirituality hold little importance in their lives
- Teens with certain psychological disorders
- Teens who have poor parental relationships
- Teens who have poor peer relationships
- Teens who have few or no future goals
- Teens who are not engaged in sports
- Teens of divorced parents
- Teens with low self-esteem and little self-confidence

She believed it was so; at least she'd been told that over and over again by her father and older brother. But deep down inside she hoped—no, she knew—it just wasn't true.

Amy, Janelle, and Dani are all sexually active teens, though each has very different reasons for being so. Amy thought she was in love and in a committed relationship; hers was consensual sex. Janelle was raped; she suffered a sexual assault, even though the drugs Tory slipped into her drink made it impossible for

RISKY RELATIONSHIPS: Casual Sex in a World of STIs

Janelle to say "no" or protest his advances. Dani's frequent, casual sex with multiple partners may have been consensual, but her promiscuous sexual activity was rooted in sexual abuse she'd suffered as a child and deep feelings of worthlessness that lingered into her teen years; she didn't think she had a choice.

Three teens, three kinds of relationships, three sets of reasons behind their sexual activities; all facing great risks.

Why Do Teens Have Sex?

The three scenarios that began this chapter illustrate some of the reasons adolescents engage in sex. One study of young women, between the ages of twelve and eighteen, who had their first sexual experience prior to age fifteen revealed the following as the primary reasons for their decisions to have intercourse:

- An older partner pressured them.
- Friends were "doing it" and they wanted to be included.
- They were curious.
- They wanted to feel grown up.

For young women whose first sexual experiences occurred after they turned seventeen years of age, the most likely reason for engaging in sex was being in love or physically attracted to their partners.

These, however, are not the only reasons teens engage in sex. Sometimes sex comes to teenagers against their wills, especially for those who are victims of child sexual abuse, rape, or sexual assault. In a study reported in the Journal of School Health, seven percent of students ages twelve through sixteen said they'd been forced to do something sexual with an adult against their wills. Another 17 percent said they were forced to

SOME TRUTHS TO REMEMBER ABOUT PORNOGRAPHY

- It's every bit as addicting as drugs and alcohol.
- It can never provide intimacy.
- It can never replace real relationships.
- It's not real. Most images are air brushed or altered.
- Models are posed to look perfect, beautiful, and sexy.
- Models used in pornography don't resemble average men and women. Many models have been surgically enhanced.
- The porn industry is a business designed to take your money.
- The porn industry takes advantage of desperate guys and girls.
- Porn models are somebody's sister, mother, daughter, brother, father, son, or friend.
- Statistically, most people addicted to porn are lonely and isolated.
- Viewing pornography can leave you disappointed with sex.
- Pornography addiction wrecks relationships and marriages.
- Pornography addiction can cost you your job.
- Some porn can lead to acting-out behaviors including sexual assault and rape.

do so with another teenager. Nineteen percent felt pressured by friends to have intercourse. And six percent, primarily males, admitted to coercing or forcing other teens to have sex.

On other occasions, teens find themselves freely engaging in sexual activity while under the influence of drugs or alcohol when they might never have intended to do so. In a national survey of teens done by the American Sexual Health Association, 29 percent of teens ages thirteen to eighteen who were sexually active (nearly one out of five) said that they had done something while high or drunk that they would never have done otherwise.

In some cases, teens have sex because they are looking for the love, acceptance, and approval they lack at home. In a study done by the Media Project, 71 percent of teens who didn't feel close to their mothers or fathers had sex between the ages of seventeen and nineteen. In another study, teens who were highly satisfied with their relationships with their parents were nearly three times less likely to engage in sex than teens who were dissatisfied with their parental relationships. Unhealthy parent-child relationships can result in teens making sexually unwise choices.

What Kinds of Sex Do Teens Have?

The term "sex" can mean many things to many people. Among adolescents it can refer to anything from solitary masturbation to oral sex to group sex to intercourse. In a 2001 study reported in Family Planning Perspectives, teen sexual activity was broken down this way: of males between the ages of fifteen and nineteen, 55 percent said they'd had vaginal intercourse; 53 percent reported being masturbated by a female; 49 percent received oral sex; 39 percent practiced oral sex on another; nine percent had engaged in homosexual sex, and 11 percent had tried anal sex.

Teenagers also seem inclined to have sex with multiple partners. Various studies report that one in five high school students will have four or more sexual partners in their lifetimes; one in ten will have seven or more partners in their lifetimes; and one in three females and one in two males will have six or more sexual partners by the time they reach age twenty-one.

Sadly, most adolescents are unaware of the health risks involved with their varied sexual practices and multiple partners.

What Risks Are Involved in Sex?

Many teens fail to realize this basic truth: When you have sex with someone, you are also having sex with everyone else your partner has been with! So if you're having sex with someone, and that someone has had sex with four other people, you are essentially having sex with all five. Not only that, you are also having sex with every partner the four others had sex with, too. When you think about it, the numbers are staggering. Just one act of sexual intercourse or oral sex could expose you to literally dozens of other people and their sexually transmitted infections (STIs).

SYMPTOMS OF COMMON STIs

If you or anyone you've had sex with has any of the following symptoms, see a doctor or clinician immediately:

- abnormal or smelly discharges from the vagina, penis, or rectum
- presence of pus or foul odors in the genital or rectal area
- vaginal or rectal bleeding
- blisters, warts, sores, or boils in the genital or rectal area
- burning sensations, itching, or irritations in the genital or rectal area
- painful intercourse
- tenderness or swelling of the genitals
- genital rashes or ulcers
- chronic vaginal yeast infections

According to a 2010 article in the *New York Times*, 80 percent of boys and 69 percent of girls ages 14 to 17 who are sexually active used a condom the last time they had sexual intercourse. The CDC also estimates that more than a quarter of all new HIV infections in the United States (the virus that leads to AIDS) occur in young people under the age of twenty-five, and most of these are acquired through unprotected sexual contact. Teenagers are risking their lives to have sex.

Fatal disease or infection isn't the only risk. Other STIs can cause permanent health issues: chlamydia, syphilis, genital her-

pes, human papillomavirus (HPV), genital warts, gonorrhea, trichomoniasis, bacterial vaginosis, scabies, and pubic lice are just some of the infections that can be transmitted through sexual contact (see the sidebar on page 69). Many cause painful sores, blistering, unbearable itching, rashes, pain or difficulty when urinating, generalized pain and tingling in the genital areas, and cervical cancer. Some diseases and infections can be treated; others cannot. All are highly contagious through sexual contact, whether oral, vaginal, or anal.

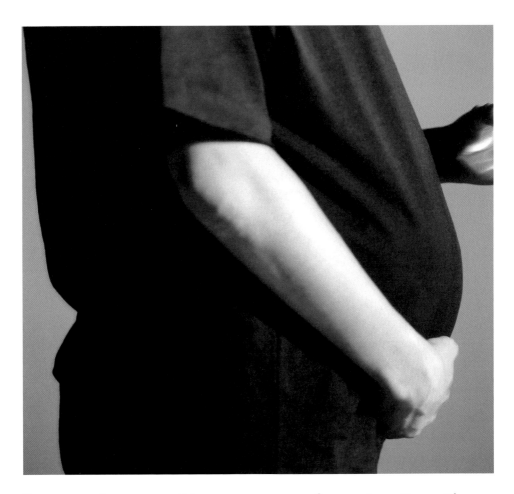

Pregnancy is one possible consequence of experimenting with a sexual relationship.

As if death and disease weren't enough, there is also the risk of unwanted pregnancy, even when condoms are used. Condoms (the rubber or latex single-finger-glove-like contraceptive that fits over the penis to prevent semen from entering the partner's body) are not foolproof; they can have microscopic holes (undetectable to the eye) that can leak, or they can break during use. According to statistics from sterlingschools.org, nearly one in ten girls between the ages of fifteen and nineteen gets pregnant each year. Of those, 56 percent will give birth. The other half will suffer early miscarriages or will abort their pregnancies.

Death, sickness, chronic disease, unwanted pregnancy—if these are all possible consequences of sex, why do teens become sexually active? In addition to the reasons discussed earlier, the bottom line is that sex is pleasurable. It feels good. And, as the teen mantra so often goes, *If it feels good, do it*. But many teens have discovered this mantra comes with a price.

The saddest part of teen sexual activity, apart from health consequences and unwanted pregnancy, is the emotional toll it takes on teens. Most regret not waiting to have sexual intercourse. A report issued by The National Campaign to Prevent Teen Pregnancy found that more than half of the boys and more than two-thirds of the girls surveyed said they wished they'd waited until they were older to have sex. More than 85 percent felt that teens should be told to wait to become sexually active until after high school. Many felt ashamed. Some felt used. Many felt taken advantage of. Most regretted the choice to be sexually active so young.

Can Sex Be Safe?

Most teens don't want to believe this, but the only 100 percent guarantee against STIs and unwanted pregnancies is abstinence. In other words, just say no to sex.

However, if you're going to have sex, use a condom, which at least provides some measure of protection. Unfortunately, as discussed earlier, they aren't foolproof; you can still get pregnant or contract diseases if the condom leaks or breaks. Alternate sexual practices (for example, engaging in oral sex instead of intercourse) cannot keep you totally safe either, since some STIs can be transmitted through the soft tissues of the mouth. Other methods of contraception (the pill, sponges, spermicides, etc.) may be effective in protecting against pregnancy, but they do nothing to prevent infection or disease.

HOW DO YOU DEFINE ABSTINENCE?

A. No vaginal intercourse, but anything else goes
B. No vaginal intercourse or anal sex, but everything else is allowed
C. No intercourse, anal sex, or oral sex, but everything else is okay
D. No intercourse, anal sex, oral sex, or fondling, but every thing else is allowed
E. No intercourse, anal or oral sex, fondling, or heavy petting, but kissing and touching is okay
F. No sexual contact at all

Confused? You should be. Abstinence is defined differently in many places. Most abstinence educators would define abstinence as C, D, E, or F, depending on the program.

COMMON STIs (OTHER THAN HIV OR AIDS)

CHLAMYDIA
   Symptoms: abnormal genital discharge; painful urination; can have few or no symptoms.
   Treatment: antibiotics.

GENITAL HERPES
   Symptoms: painful blisters or open sores in the genital area; tingling or burning sensations in the legs, buttocks, or genital region. Sores usually disappear within two to three weeks, but can return.
   Treatment: Drugs help the symptoms, but the herpes virus remains in the body for life.

GENITAL WARTS
   Symptoms: small, hard, painless bumps in the vaginal area, on the penis, or around the anus; can develop a fleshy, cauliflower-like appearance.
   Treatment: topical drugs applied to the skin; freezing; injections; or surgical removal.

GONORRHEA
   Symptoms: a discharge from the vagina or penis and painful or difficult urination.
   Treatment: penicillin or newer antibiotics for drug-resistant strains.

SYPHILIS
   Symptoms: a painless, open sore that usually appears on the penis or around or in the vagina. It can also occur near the mouth, anus, or on the hands.
   Treatment: penicillin; treatment can take years.

CORRECT CONDOM USE

If condoms are used incorrectly, they can slip, leak, or break resulting in little or no protection from disease or pregnancy. To use condoms most effectively, seven steps are involved:

- Step One: Use a new condom for each sexual act.
- Step Two: Handle the condom carefully to avoid damage from fingernails, teeth, or other sharp objects.
- Step Three: Put the condom on after the penis is erect and before any genital contact occurs with the partner.
- Step Four: Make sure no air is trapped in the tip of the condom.
- Step Five: Use adequate lubrication during intercourse.
- Step Six: Use only water-based lubricants with latex condoms.
- Step Seven: Hold the condom firmly against the base of the penis during withdrawal, making sure to withdraw while the penis is still erect.

(Adapted from a Henry J. Kaiser Family Foundation Fact Sheet.)

You will have to a take a look at the facts and make your own decision; this is a very personal realm of life, and only you can decide what to do. But these are the facts: the only way to stay sexually healthy and safe is to abstain from sex until you are older and in a committed, monogamous relationship with someone who hasn't had other partners. Only virgins marrying virgins who remain faithfully monogamous are 100 percent sexually safe.

If you do choose to be sexually active, however, there are steps you can take to reduce your sexual risks (remember, these are not guarantees):

- Know your partner well (health status, who else he or she has been with).
- Always use condoms (made of latex) for oral, anal, or vaginal sex.
- Don't do drugs.
- Don't get drunk.
- Don't accept open container drinks from anyone (they could be drugged). Accept drinks only if they are sealed or if you've seen them opened and poured.
- Don't put yourself in unsafe situations. Use your common sense.
- If you've been sexually abused, tell someone in authority. Get help.
- If you've been raped or drugged, get medical attention immediately.

High-risk sexual behavior does not have to be the norm for adolescents. Like drug use, most sexual behaviors are a choice. You can choose not to have sex at all, or if you've been sexually active in the past, you can choose something called "secondary virginity" (essentially saying that from now on you will choose to abstain). If you decide to be sexually active, you can make the choices listed above to reduce your risks.

Discovering your sexual identity is all part of becoming an adult, but this can be a healthy or unhealthy process. It can be high risk or no risk. It's all up to you.

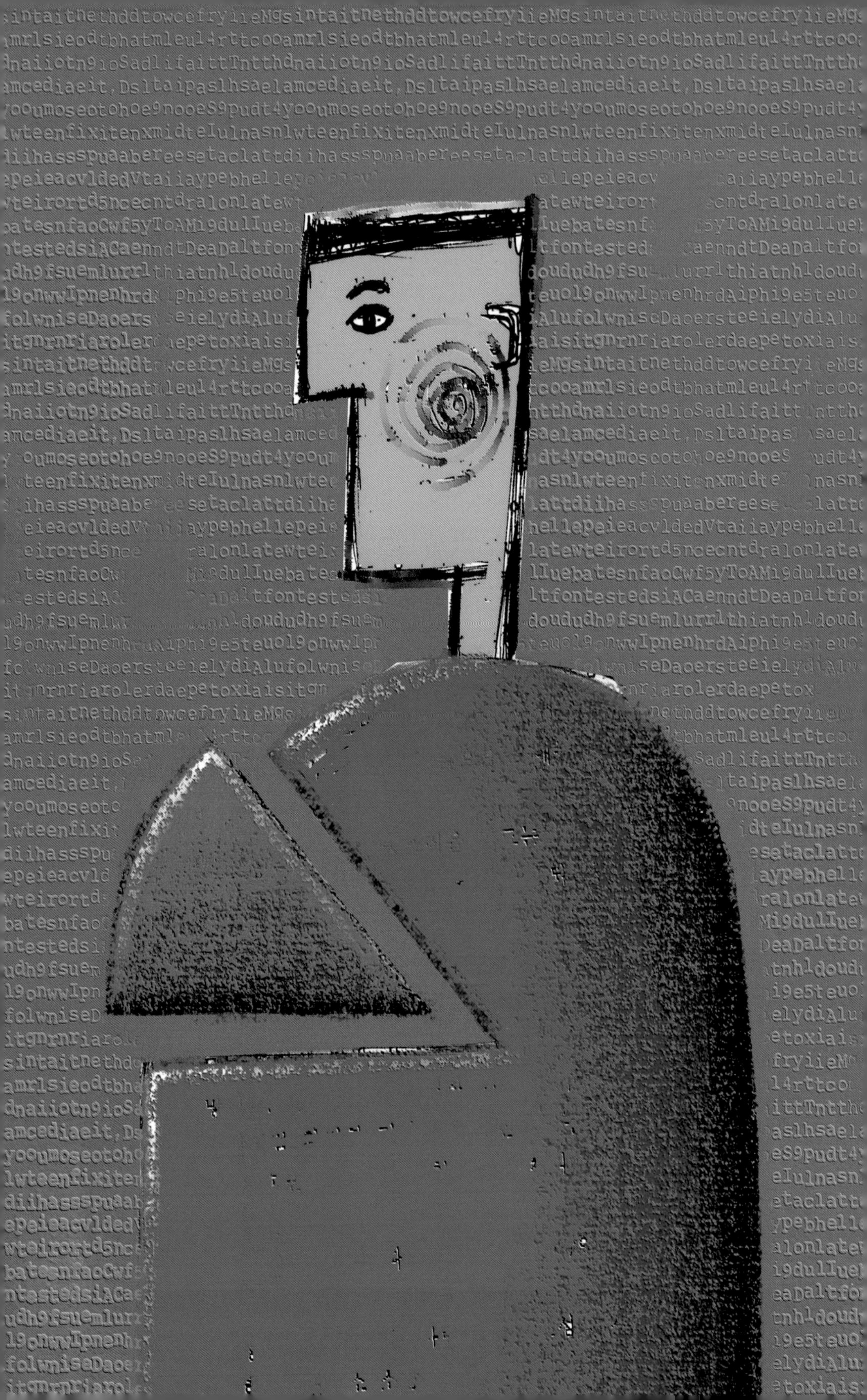

4

SELF-INJURY:
It's Not What You Think

Can you imagine slicing your stomach with a razor blade or carving a design in your arm? How about burning your fingertips with a cigarette butt or scorching your palms with a lighter? Do you think you could ever intentionally break a finger, an arm, a foot, or a leg, just because you wanted to?

Most of the following teens didn't think they could either. Until they started. Then they couldn't stop. Here's how their journeys with self-injury began (told in their own words):

Case One

I began to SI when I was ten years old. I didn't even realize what I was doing at first. I was just really mad at my mom and started scratching my arm until I could feel the blood seeping through. It felt really good. It was a release of all the pain I'd kept inside. I found a new friend that I could turn to, and so I continued to seek out this new companion. I began by cutting my ankles. Then I started cutting my thighs. It helped me cope with things I couldn't control. One day a friend asked me if I wanted to stop, and I said no. I'm still cutting. It has become something I need in my life.

HOW CAN I TELL IF A FRIEND IS SELF-INJURING?

- Does your friend have cuts or scars on her arms or legs?
- Does your friend try to keep you from seeing her scars?
- Does your friend wear long pants and long-sleeve shirts even in hot weather?
- Does your friend offer lame explanations for her injuries ("The cat scratched me.")?
- Is your friend depressed, angry, under pressure, or having a hard time?

If you answered yes to these questions, your friend may be self-injuring. Talk with her about it in a nonjudgmental way.

Case Two

I am a sixteen-year-old theatre student who goes to a magnet high school for students gifted in the arts. I do not have a crummy or dysfunctional family. My parents are wonderful; they love me and I love them. I have it together as far as my friends are concerned. I have a good life.

But I was raped by a boyfriend when I was fourteen. I'm not sure if that's what made me SI the first time. It wasn't until after I was raped that I started. But one night, while I was home alone, I was upset, so I picked up a knife and began slicing my arms. I felt this relief like I'd never felt before. I felt that I had found a way to control the pain I was experiencing. I liked the fact that I could control my life and feelings again.

Self-injury was first described in medical literature as early as 1938. Then it was called self-mutilative behavior (SMB).

Case Three

I'm fourteen years old, and I've been self-injuring for almost a year now. I know that compared to a lot of people that isn't much, but I'm already hooked. I was hooked the first time I tried it. It's like a drug addiction, and I can't stop. I would like to quit, but throwing the blades away isn't enough. I've tried that, but I always find more sharp things in the house to play with. I'm currently trying another way to stop that seems to work better: distractions.

These teens reflect some of the paradoxes of self-injury: they hate and like what they do. They want and don't want to stop. They cut, burn, and bruise themselves, but they don't want to kill themselves. They find shame and comfort in their scars.

What Is Self-Injury (SI)?

Self-injury (SI), also known as self-injurious behavior (SIB), self-mutilation, cutting, self-abuse, and para-suicidal behavior, is a widely misunderstood phenomenon characterized by repeated, deliberate, non-lethal harming of one's body. The greatest misunderstanding about SI is the assumption that self-injurers want to die and that their self-injurious behaviors are just veiled attempts at suicide. Not so, say the founders of S.A.F.E. Alternatives (Self Abuse Finally Ends), a nationally recognized treatment program, professional network, and resource base committed to ending self-injurious behavior. They describe the reasons for self-injury this way:

Self-injurers commonly report that they feel empty inside, over or under stimulated, unable to express their feelings, lonely, not understood by others and fearful of intimate relationships and adult responsibilities. Self-injury is their way to cope with or relieve painful or hard-to-express feelings and is generally not a suicide attempt.

In other words, self-injurers harm themselves in order to help themselves; they aren't trying to kill themselves.

Who Self-Injures?

According to Mental Health America, about two million people in the U.S. self-injure. Most are females, but males SI, too. Self-injurers typically start harming themselves in their pre-teen or teenage years, and continue for five to ten years (longer without treatment). Nearly 50 percent of self-injurers were sexually abused as children, and some, but not all, have related diagnosable psychological disorders, including BORDERLINE PERSONALITY DISORDER, BIPOLAR DISORDER, major depression, anxiety disorders, and various psychoses such as SCHIZOPHRENIA.

Self-injurers come in all shapes and sizes: black, white, Asian, Hispanic, and just about any other nationality, skin color, or culture in the world; rich and poor; high school scholars and junior high dropouts; heterosexuals, homosexuals, and bisexuals; fat and thin people, tall and short people, athletic and klutzy people; people from all faiths and religious backgrounds; success stories and failures. Outward issues do not determine whether or not

While many do, some self-injurers do not feel any pain when they cut or burn themselves; the predominant feeling is relief.

A CRY FOR HELP

Though her biographies recount her well-known struggles with bulimia, it wasn't until the months preceding her death that the late Princess Diana, the Duchess of Wales, confessed that she had thrown herself down a flight of stairs, had purposefully fallen into a glass display case, and had cut herself with razors, penknives, and lemon cutters. One of the most photographed people in the entire world, beautiful Lady Diana, shy, gentle, compassionate Diana, loved and admired by millions, was a self-injurer. Why? As she said in her own words in an interview with the British Broadcasting System (BBC), "You have so much pain inside yourself, you try and hurt yourself on the outside because you need help." The Princess's attempts at self-injury were a silent cry for help. Some self-injurers have called it the "silent scream."

someone becomes a self-injurer; it has more to do with an inward inability to express feelings or cope with strong emotions.

Why Do People Self-Injure?

The primary reason people self-injure is to relieve emotional pain. It's an extreme coping mechanism some people use to get through times of stress, anxiety, conflict, disappointment, failure, or heartache. Many self-injurers have never developed the ability to feel or express emotions in a healthy way. Self-injury provides relief from the pressure of pent-up feelings. As one teen self-injurer put it, "I felt my emotional pain drain away with

SELF-INJURY: It's Not What You Think

my blood. It's as though punching a hole in my skin deflated this balloon of intense, overwhelming feelings. The air of pain came out slowly, and the release only lasted a short time, but it still gave me much-needed relief."

Other self-injurers harm themselves in order to feel something, to feel anything at all. They are numb emotionally. Physical pain helps the self-injurer acknowledge his or her emotional pain. One self-injurer described it this way: "It's like I was dead inside. Cutting reminded me that I was still alive and that I could still feel something."

Some self-injurers are punishing themselves or expressing self-hatred. They don't want to die; they just feel the need to blame, criticize, and punish themselves. This is particularly true of those self-injurers who were abused sexually, physically, or emotionally as young children. They replay imaginary videotapes of messages they heard from their abusers in their minds over and over again: you're so worthless; it's your fault; you deserve to be punished; you're bad; you have to pay. In self-injurers' minds, cutting themselves serves two purposes: it punishes them with pain and allows some of their badness to seep out with their blood. It's a way for them to make up for their badness.

In another paradox of SI, some self-injurers harm themselves in order to pay special attention to themselves. It gives them an excuse to indulge in self-care. They can wash and bandage their injuries afterward; they can treat themselves gently; they can take time to pamper themselves. This is the least common reason for self-injury.

Most people who self-injure, regardless of their reasons, can find help to stop SI.

Treatment Options

The first and most important step self-injurers can take is to decide to stop hurting themselves. This decision can only be made if the self-injurer has developed other ways to handle her overwhelming emotions. How can someone addicted to SI develop other coping mechanisms?

- Get professional help. Find a therapist, counselor, psychologist, or psychiatrist that specializes in treating SI, and go to him or her. SI is every bit as addictive as drugs or pornography or tobacco. Overcoming this addiction will require the help of a trained practitioner.

THE HIDDEN DANGERS OF SI

- addiction
- infection
- permanent scarring
- escalating injuries (requiring more serious injuries to produce the desired effect)
- misjudging the severity of an injury (causing more harm than intended)
- possibility of permanent injury
- possibility of long-term health effects
- possibility of unintentional suicide
- possible spread of blood-borne disease (HIV or hepatitis)
- increased desperation over lack of control

- Get evaluated by a mental health profes-sional for other contributing psychological disorders. SI is often symptomatic of other conditions, especially borderline personality disorder and OBSESSIVE-COMPULSIVE DISORDER. Some of these disorders, even SI itself, can be rooted in imbalances of chemicals in the brain that can be treated effectively by prescription drugs. Only a licensed clinician (an advanced practice nurse, a psychiatrist or other M.D.) can prescribe these medications.

Many self-injurers can seek professional help success-fully as outpatients. Some, however, especially if their SI is severe or psy-chotic, may need in-patient hospitalization for a short period of time.

Some self-injurers find help in self-help strategies: distraction (finding something else to do); making sure they are not alone; doing something creative with their hands (making cookies, kneading bread dough, knitting, playing the guitar or piano, journaling, drawing, or painting); listening to uplifting or soothing music; trying self-talk (telling themselves "no" or evaluating pros and cons); calling a friend; using ice (instead of cutting), snapping rubber bands (instead of cutting); exercising; going for a walk; petting or holding a pet; or going to the movies, and so on.

According to the Fulshear Academy, the most effective treatment strategies will include a combination of professional help (including medications and COGNITIVE BEHAVIORAL THERAPY), self-help strategies, and interpersonal support. Every person who struggles with SI needs at least one friend or family member who understands, who is there for her, and will not contribute to her shame.

TYPES OF SELF-INJURIOUS BEHAVIORS

- cutting, carving, or slicing skin
- burning or branding
- biting or chewing
- whipping
- scratching or rubbing to point of abrasion
- puncturing skin with foreign objects
- inserting objects into body openings
- beating, hitting, punching, or slapping (self or objects)
- picking or pulling at skin, scabs, or pimples
- head banging
- hair pulling
- infecting oneself or interfering with healing
- intentionally bruising or breaking bones
- starving or bingeing and purging
- excessive body piercing
- excessive tattooing
- extreme physical risk-taking
- engaging in unhealthy sexual activity

How Should I React if Someone I Know Self-Injures?

SI can bring out a host of emotions from people who don't understand the condition: shock, revulsion, anger, fear, confusion, disgust, shame, and condemnation, among others. Self-injurers have already felt these things about themselves, too. Especially shame.

SELF-INJURY: It's Not What You Think

HOW DO I KNOW IF I'M READY TO STOP SI?

Ask yourself these questions (the more "yes" answers; the more ready you are):

- Do I want to stop?
- Do I have a network of supportive professionals, friends, and family members already in place that will help me?
- Can I talk to at least three people honestly and comfortably about my SI?
- Do I have at least three people I can call to be with if I'm tempted to self-injure?
- Have I gotten rid of (or safely locked away) all the things I use to hurt myself?
- Do I have a place to go if I have to leave my house to keep from hurting myself?
- Have I signed (or am I ready to sign) a contract stating that I will no longer hurt myself?
- Have I given signed copies of this contract to at least two other people?
- Am I willing to try alternate coping strategies, including medication?
- Have I listed at least fifteen positive things I can do instead of SI?
- Am I willing to admit, accept, face, and work through my feelings without SI?

Shame is what makes self-injurers wear long sleeves all summer long or long pants when it should be shorts weather. Shame keeps them trying to cover their scars and hiding their injuries so no one else will know. Shame is an incredibly strong, self-condemning emotion that can keep self-injurers feeling badly about themselves and trapped in a cycle of self-destruction.

One of the best things you can do for someone you know who self-injures is to accept him as he is without adding to his shame. Stay calm. Allow him to talk about his addiction with you. Try not to react emotionally to what he tells you, but do react medically if there is a need (take him to a doctor or hospital if his injuries are severe enough). Offer to stay with him if he feels an episode coming on (most won't cut themselves in front of other people). Offer to do things together. If you are both teens, find an adult you can trust. Encourage the self-injurer to get help. Let your friend know you care, even if you don't know what to do.

Remember, no one can make self-injurers stop hurting themselves. That's a choice only they can make for themselves. It's a choice, however, that they may need support to reach, either through professional help or the assistance of a few good friends.

Another Kind of SI

One last kind of SI will be discussed in the next chapter: eating disorders. These attempts at self-harm, whether starvation (anorexia), bingeing and purging (bulimia), or extreme overeating, are too important, too widespread, too deadly, and too complicated to squeeze into this chapter. They need a chapter all their own. Remember, however, that they, too, are silent cries for help. Eating disorders need to be handled with every bit as much compassion, patience, and understanding as other forms of SI.

5

Eating Disorders:
Pursuing Perfection in
an Air-Brushed World

"It's so hard to wake up in the morning and be afraid to look in the mirror."

"I live with a tiny voice inside my head that tells me how fat and disgusting I am."

"I don't want to be normal. I want to be perfect."

"To me, it's not about my looks; it's that I look inside and find myself lacking."

LESSER KNOWN EATING OR RELATED DISORDERS

- anorexia athletica (compulsive exercising)
- body dysmorphic disorder (BDD) (obsessively viewing self as inordinately ugly)
- orthorexia nervosa (obsessing over "pure" food)
- night-eating syndrome (eating most calories at night)
- gourmand syndrome (obsessing over "fine" food)
- pica (craving non-food items like dirt, paint, plaster, chalk, etc.)
- chewing and spitting (tasting, chewing, then spitting out food, but not eating it)

"If anyone had told me last year that in a year's time I'd be puking three-to-five times a day, I would have told them they were crazy, and I would have been wrong."

"Whenever anyone says to me 'I wish I could be as skinny as you,' I just want to smack them! Don't they know that once you start down this road, it has you for life?!"

These are all comments from real teens who struggle with very real eating disorders. Many of these adolescents came from "normal" homes with loving families. Some were athletes, some were overachievers in school, some were beautiful, and others less so. But none of them was grossly overweight when they began to view themselves as "fat" or "chubby" or "solid" or "thick." In fact, most can recall standing in front of their mirrors as young as five, six, or seven years of age and thinking they were overweight.

Suicide & Self-Destructive Behaviors

What could make girls so young see themselves as "fat"? Consider this: The average American girl between the ages of three and ten owns eleven Barbie® dolls. More than one billion of Mattel's Barbie® dolls have been sold since 1959 (including the dolls of her friends and family), and if placed head-to-toe, according to one estimate, the total dolls sold would circle the Earth more than seven times! Girls all over the world have been led to believe that "pretty" means looking just like Barbie®, the doll she has played with since she can remember. Yet, according to an Associated Press report, Barbie's® measurements, if she were enlarged to real life size, would be a thirty-eight-inch bust, an eighteen-inch waist, and thirty-four-inch hips—proportions that some anatomists claim are anatomically impossible.

After years of public uproar over Barbie's® unrealistic design, Barbie® had a makeover in 1998: her measurements, if she were enlarged to be 5 feet and 6 inches tall, became 36-21-33. The new dimensions gave Barbie® a flatter chest and wider waist, but according to one statistician, the likelihood of a girl ever developing a figure like Barbie's, even the new version, is less than one in a hundred thousand. Yet advertisements and television programming make girls think this is the ideal.

Media messages, fashion images, consumer advertising, television programming, and toys convey a super-skinny image

In 1997, two college wrestlers died when they tried drastic weight loss methods to reach lower target weights for their respective wrestling teams. Both wore rubber suits while working out in hot rooms in an effort to lose more body fluids. One died of kidney failure and heart malfunction, the other died of cardiac arrest after working out on an exercise bike and refusing to drink liquids. They died trying to lose four to six pounds.

EATING DISORDERS

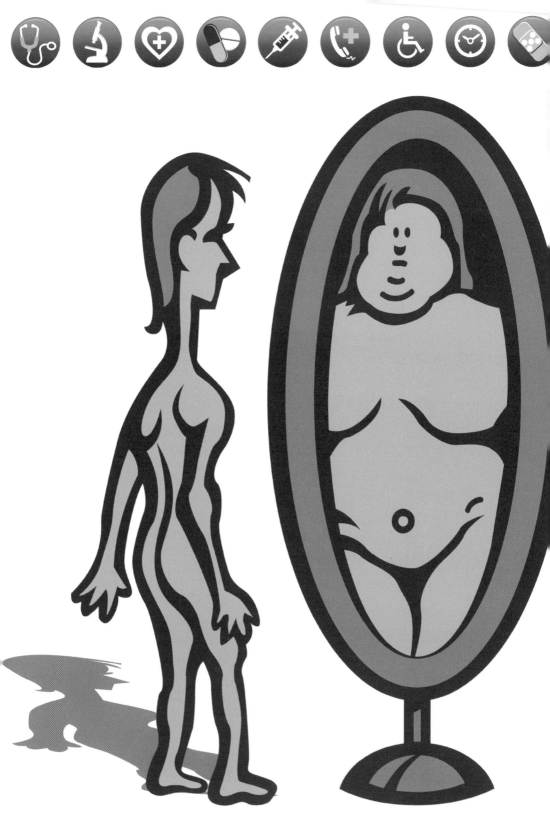

Suicide & Self-Destructive Behaviors

The average American woman is 5'4" tall and weighs 140 pounds. The average American model is 5'11" tall and weighs 117 pounds. Most fashion models are thinner than 98 percent of American women.

as the norm. In a study of Saturday morning toy commercials aimed at girls, researchers found that 50 percent of the ads commented on physical appearance, while none of the ads aimed at boys in the same time period commented on attractiveness ("Media Effects on Girls: Body Image and Gender Identity"). Another survey, conducted by Girl Scouts of America, revealed that nine out of ten teen girls feel pressure to be skinny. But it isn't just media messages that can damage a girl's body image; less than-sensitive family members can make young people think badly about themselves, too.

One seventeen-year-old from Virginia recalls her older brothers calling her "thunder thighs" when she was only nine years old. She started dieting by age ten.

Another teen describes how ashamed and mortified she felt when her mother said things like, "You're not overweight; you're just pleasantly plump." Even as a rail-thin, severely underweight sixteen-year-old, she still hears pleasantly plump every time she looks in the mirror.

When Alex's stepfather moved from calling her "sturdy" and "athletic" to calling her "butter butt," the thirteen-year-old started making herself throw up after she ate so she wouldn't gain weight.

Media messages, name-calling, impossible standards—these can all contribute to a teenager's development of an unhealthy body image, but they don't necessarily cause eating disorders.

STATISTICS FOR DIETERS

- Every day, 28,493 Canadians start diets.
- Ninety-three percent of all women feel anxiety about how they look. About 80 percent of all girls have tried at least one diet by age eighteen.
- Eighty percent of all dieters regain their lost weight after two years.
- Americans spend over forty billion dollars on dieting and diet-related products each year.

They contribute to inappropriate eating habits, but true eating disorders are often caused by deeper emotional and biological problems.

What Are Eating Disorders?

Most North Americans have heard about miracle diets, weight loss programs, diet shakes, low-calorie snack bars, reduced-fat foods, and the next "ten easy steps to losing ten pounds by summer vacation" plan. Dieting is a common practice for many people. But going on a short-term diet to lose those extra five or ten pounds is not the same thing as developing an eating disorder.

An eating disorder is an obsession with food, weight, and self-body-image that results in a person's developing eating habits severe enough to damage his or her physical health and emotional well-being.

Sixteen-year-old Tasha's fingers and toes turned blue, her hair fell out, she felt tired and dizzy all the time, and her period stopped, all because she was starving herself to stay thin.

Many young women in North America feel pressure to conform to a certain body type.

Sean, a fourteen-year-old wrestler, battled chronic sore throats, painful heartburn, and rotting teeth because he made himself vomit frequently to "make weight" for the wrestling team.

As a college freshman, eighteen-year-old Marita used cocaine to lose weight, took laxatives to rid her body of unwanted bulk, and started running excessively to get rid of body fluid. Only after nearly dying from dehydration did this teen realize that she might have a problem.

In their obsession to be thin, people with eating disorders put their bodies at great risk, and can do great harm. What makes them behave this way?

Causes of Eating Disorders

Like the destructive behaviors we looked at in the previous chapters, this high-risk behavior can be caused by several things. The National Eating Disorders Association identifies four main groups of causes:

- psychological factors (low self-esteem, feelings of inadequacy, depression, anxiety, loss of feelings of control, anger, loneliness, etc.)
- interpersonal factors (troubled family life, difficulty expressing feelings, history of being teased or abused)
- social factors (cultural pressures, emphasis on the "perfect body," narrow definitions of beauty that include only certain body shapes, types, and sizes, cultural norms that value external appearance over inner qualities)
- other factors (possible biochemical, neurological, or biological causes)

The U.S. National Institute of Mental Health (NIMH) defines eating disorders as "real, treatable medical illnesses. They fre-

Suicide & Self-Destructive Behaviors

quently coexist with other illnesses such as depression, substance abuse, or anxiety disorders." The NIMH recognizes that eating disorders aren't just about food. Like SI, they're often an attempt by the affected person to express painful emotions or to take control of something when everything else feels out of control.

And just as SI comes in many forms, so do eating disorders.

Types of Eating Disorders

The NIMH identifies the three most common types of eating disorders as anorexia nervosa, bulimia nervosa, and binge-eating disorder. Doctors have identified many other lesser known eating disorders (see the sidebar on page 88), but this chapter will focus on these three.

FAMOUS PEOPLE WHO HAVE HAD EATING DISORDERS

- Princess Diana
- Geri Haliwell
- Jamie-Lynn Sigler
- Paula Abdul
- Jane Fonda
- Joan Rivers
- Sally Field
- Courtney Thorne-Smith
- Tracey Gold
- Justine Bateman
- Cathy Rigby

EATING DISORDERS

WARNING SIGNS THAT A FRIEND MAY HAVE AN EATING DISORDER

- She's obsessed with weight and food.
- She counts fat grams and calories.
- She avoids eating with you.
- When she eats with you, she makes frequent trips to the bathroom.
- She wears baggy clothes.
- You've seen or heard her vomit after a meal.
- You've seen her take laxatives, fluid pills, appetite suppressants, or diet aids.
- She always talks about how fat she is.
- She works out too much.
- She gets light-headed, dizzy, faints, or complains about being cold.

The first, anorexia nervosa, is characterized by an intense fear of gaining weight or getting fat even though a person is extremely underweight. This fear, coupled with an inaccurate perception of self, results in an extreme reluctance to eat or a cessation of eating altogether. Anorexics will often avoid meals, pick at foods but not eat, weigh themselves obsessively, and may use other weight control methods (extreme exercise, laxative or ENEMA use, DIURETIC abuse). The American Academy of Child and Adolescent Psychiatry identifies the typical teen anorexic as "a perfectionist and a high achiever in school," but who has low

Suicide & Self-Destructive Behaviors

self-esteem and who "irrationally believ[es] she is fat regardless of how thin she becomes."

Anorexics can do immense harm to their bodies. They are at great risk for extreme weight loss, malnutrition, brain damage, low blood pressure, stomach and digestive problems, heart damage, heart failure, irregular menstrual cycles, stopping of menstrual cycles, development of excessively dry skin and brittle nails, the development of fine hair (called lanugo) all over their bodies, and extreme hair loss. Anorexic teens can also be at risk for slowed growth and development, irregular heartbeat, complete gastrointestinal shutdown, and bone strength problems.

This eating disorder can also be fatal. According to U.S. New Health, "approximately 86 deaths in 100,000 among 15-to-24-year-olds are attributed to anorexia nervosa."

The NIMH estimates that 0.6 percent of the American population will suffer from anorexia nervosa in their lifetime, with the vast majority beginning in their teen years. Though guys can have the disease, girls are three times more likely to experience anorexia. The National Association of Anorexia Nervosa and Associated Disorders (ANAD) ranks anorexia as the third most common illness among adolescents.

Bulimia Nervosa is the second most common eating disorder. Symptoms for this disorder differ from the first. In this case, the bulimic doesn't fear food; she "binges" on it. She consumes an excessive amount of food in a short period of time, and then "purges" the food from her system either by making herself vomit before the food is digested, or by using enemas or laxatives to rid herself of digested food. The bulimic's fear isn't food; it's weight gain.

To be truly considered bulimic, a person's binge/purge cycles must occur twice a week for at least three months, the person

must not be able to control her behavior, and she must seem obsessed with food, her weight, and body shape.

Because bulimics vomit so much, they put themselves at risk for different health issues than anorexics. Stomach acid can damage the esophagus, enlarge glands in the throat, and wear away tooth enamel, leaving the bulimic with rotting teeth and gums. Frequent vomiting can also damage the stomach, cause ulcers, damage the pancreas, cause life-threatening dehydration, and throw off the entire body's chemical metabolism, putting the patient at risk for heart failure or death.

The ANAD estimates that slightly more girls will have bulimia nervosa in their lifetimes than those who have anorexia nervosa, though the difference is less than one percent. In both cases, the driving desire is to be thin. Not all eating disorders, however, are rooted in an obsession with thinness. The third most common eating disorder has nothing to do with weight at all.

Binge-eating disorder includes excessive eating, or "binges," as bulimia nervosa does, but the binges are not followed by the need to purge. People with binge-eating disorder often experience episodes of out-of-control eating, even when the person feels uncomfortably full. They can eat large amounts of food even when they don't feel hungry, they might eat alone because they are embarrassed by how much they eat, they might consume their food faster than most people, and they may feel disgusted with themselves or depressed because of their overeating.

To be considered a binge-eater, the University of Pittsburgh Medical Center (UPMC) notes that, in addition to the eating habits described above, the person must be upset about his behavior, must not regularly purge or fast, and must binge at least two days per week for a minimum of six months.

WHAT TO DO IF YOU THINK A FRIEND HAS AN EATING DISORDER

1. Be supportive.
2. Express your concern ("I'm worried that you didn't eat lunch today; are you okay?")
3. Avoid conversations about weight, body, and food.
4. Do your research. Find resources or organizations you can direct your friend to.
5. Gently ask your friend if she's skipping meals, purging, or taking laxatives.
6. Offer to go with her to talk to her parents, a school counselor, or her doctor.
7. If your friend denies she has a problem, talk to an adult you trust about your concern.
8. Let your friend know you're there for her no matter what.
9. Don't ignore your suspicions. Eating disorders can kill if left untreated.
10. If your friend shows dangerous symptoms (passes out, is disoriented or confused), get help or get her to a doctor immediately.

The health risks for binge-eaters are primarily excessive weight gain and the health risks that come with being overweight: excessive fatigue, joint pain, high cholesterol, high blood pressure, gallbladder disease, heart disease, and increased risk for TYPE II DIABETES.

Treatment Options

All eating disorders have a psychological component that requires the attention of a psychologically trained professional. And because all eating disorders are potentially fatal, it's important for those with eating disorders to get help. Treatment strategies will vary, however, depending on what type of disorder a person has and how severe her disorder is. A severely underweight person with anorexia nervosa, for example, will have to be put on an eating plan that will slowly restore her to a healthy body weight, while treating the underlying emotional and psychological factors that caused her disorder. A severely overweight person who struggles with binge-eating disorder may still have to address underlying psychological and emo-

EATING DISORDER TREATMENT: A TEAM APPROACH

The American Academy of Child and Adolescent Psychiatry encourages a team approach to treating eating disorders. This "team" should include a psychiatric professional, individual therapy, family therapy, a family doctor, a nutritionist, and medication. Teens with eating disorders often have other underlying psychiatric problems, including depression, obsessive-compulsive disorder, anxiety, or substance abuse. The eating disorder cannot be successfully treated unless the other issues are addressed as well. A team can work together to address them all.

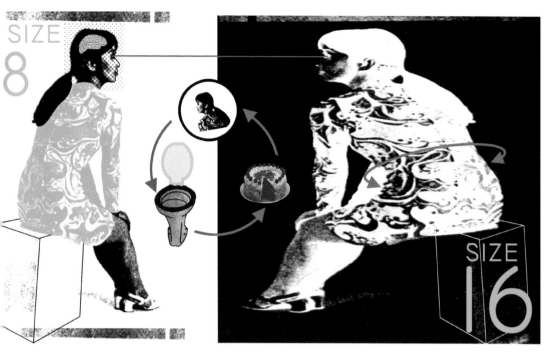

tional issues, but his physical treatment plan's goal will be to reduce his weight.

Depending on severity, some people with eating disorders may need to begin their treatment plans while staying in a hospital. Others manage their disorders as daily outpatients. Still others thrive in once-a-week support group settings. How an eating disorder is treated is best determined by a licensed professional, which is why it is so important for those with eating disorders to seek professional help.

The Best Treatment Option: Prevention

Perhaps the best treatment option for eating disorders is prevention. Take time to learn about healthy eating habits and guidelines. Ignore cultural messages that say you need to be ultra-thin to be attractive or healthy. Focus on inner qualities

Suicide & Self-Destructive Behaviors

and strengths rather than on external appearances. Learn to value people for who they are, not what they look like. Communicate affirming messages of acceptance and approval to yourself, your friends, and your loved ones. Resist the urge to tease someone about her appearance; she may have a medical condition you know nothing about; respect individual differences. Pursue overall health and fitness, not an image or a number on a scale. And realize that the media images you see every day are lies. REAL people don't look like the people you see on TV.

It's far easier to prevent an eating disorder than it is to treat one. What steps can you take today, this week, or this month to choose a healthier lifestyle? Your choices may be more important than you think.

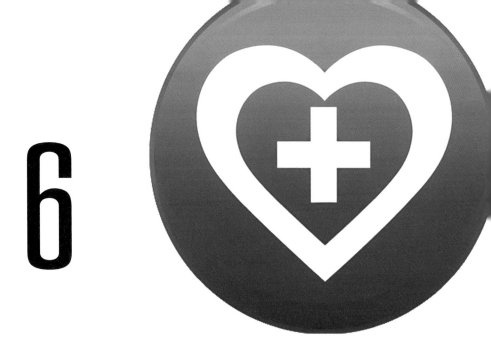

6

Suicide: A Permanent Fix for Temporary Problems

In the time it has taken you to read this book, assuming it's taken you roughly two hours, one young person between the ages of fifteen and twenty-five will have successfully completed suicide somewhere in the United States. In the time it took him to take his life, between eight and twenty-five others will have attempted, but not completed, suicide. By the end of this day, another twelve young people will be dead by their own hands.

Suicide is the second leading cause of death among Canadian youth ages ten to twenty-four, and is the third leading cause of death for the same age group in the United States. It is the second leading cause of death among U.S. college students. According to the National Alliance on Mental Illness, suicide takes more teenage and young adult lives than cancer, heart disease, AIDS, birth defects, stroke, and chronic lung disease combined.

Sadly, teen suicide rates appear to be rising. More kids seem to be taking their lives, or attempting to do so, each year. Young people are at greater risk for suicide today than at any other time in U.S. history.

Which Teens Are Most Likely to Attempt Suicide?

Focus Adolescent Services, a widespread outreach program to troubled teens, identifies the following as major risk factors for suicide among young people. Teens who have or do these things are the most likely to attempt suicide:

- depression
- substance abuse (alcohol or other drugs)
- behavioral problems (fighting with parents, breaking the law, etc.)
- gun availability (more guns are used in suicides than homicides each year)
- previous suicide attempts
- recent traumatic event
- other psychological disorders

Other organizations describe additional risk factors: unsupportive family backgrounds, relationship troubles, poor coping skills, psychiatric illnesses, aggressive or disruptive behaviors,

Suicide & Self-Destructive Behaviors

history of abuse, chronic physical illness, poor body image, eating problems, feelings of worthlessness or helplessness, recent failure or disappointment, perfectionistic tendencies.

Sound familiar? Most of these have also been factors in a teen's choice to abuse drugs or alcohol, to self-injure, to participate in unsafe sex, or to develop eating disorders. The very same things that can drive a teenager to the self-destructive behaviors discussed so far in this book can also drive him to suicide.

Another factor is bullying.

Bullying and Suicide

On May 6, 1998, ninety-eight-pound sixth-grader Jared High was brutally assaulted in his middle school gym by a 170-pound eighth grader with a reputation for assaulting other students. For eight full minutes the bully slammed the smaller boy against walls, punched him, and kicked him in the stomach, back, shoulders, and head. When the younger student was finally able to escape the building, the bully followed, throwing him up against the exterior brick walls. Jared's chiropractor said later, after looking at the boy's post-assault X rays, that it looked as though he'd been in a major car accident.

In the months that followed, Jared suffered many physical and psychological symptoms stemming from the assault: nau-

Among fifteen to nineteen-year-olds, more teen girls try to commit suicide each year than teen boys. But teen boys in this age bracket are more likely to complete their suicide attempts than girls. Eighty-one percent of successful suicides in adolescents ages ten to twenty-four were committed by males.

(Centers for Disease Control and Prevention, 2012)

Suicide & Self-Destructive Behaviors

Substance abuse is involved in nearly half of all suicide attempts. Twenty percent of all suicides involve alcohol abusers.

(National Mental Health Association)

sea, vomiting, stomach pain, diar-rhea, sleep problems, chiro-practic issues, depression, and probable post-traumatic stress disorder.

Jared completed suicide on September 29, 1998, less than five months after he was attacked, and only six days after his thirteenth birthday.

Depression

Psychiatrists are beginning to establish a link between bullying and suicide through the factor they have in common: depression. Victims of bullying often struggle with feelings of helplessness, depression, and low self-esteem, all of which can make the victim pursue self-destructive coping mechanisms.

FACTORS REDUCING SUICIDE RISK

- a strong sense of family (for all youth)
- emotional well-being (stronger for girls)
- high grade-point average (stronger for guys)

FIVE COMMON MYTHS ABOUT SUICIDE

1. Only depressed or crazy people commit suicide.
2. Successful, popular people don't commit suicide.
3. People who say they want to die are only looking for attention.
4. Most suicides occur without warning.
5. A person who has tried suicide won't try it again.

Usually, however, the teen that turns to suicide experiences some sort of "trigger" or final straw that pushes him over the edge. It can be, among other things, a break-up with a girlfriend, the outing of his sexual preferences, failing a big exam, or the decision by his parents to divorce.

These traumatic life events are difficult enough to handle, but youth with depression or other underlying issues may not have the resources to deal with their pain. It isn't so much that these teens want to die; it's that they want relief from their hurting.

The Short-Term Perspective

Complicating the issue is most teenagers' inability to look at life from a long-term perspective. They don't tend to think in the big-picture or wide-screen view. The extreme pain they're experiencing right now seems to them like it will go on forever. It won't, of course, but it seems that way. Some teens can't believe that things will ever get better or that they will ever feel any differently.

Suicide & Self-Destructive Behaviors

Sadly, this short-sighted perspective leads the hurting teen to try a permanent solution to what is actually a very temporary problem. These desperate adolescents know they can't live with their pain forever, which they assume they will have to do, so they end their lives.

But how many teenagers actually stay in high school forever?

How many take the same test every day for the next thirty years?

How many fourteen-year-olds stay fourteen for more than twelve months?

How many watch their parents go through the same divorce for decades?

PSYCHOLOGICAL DISORDERS COMMON TO SUICIDE ATTEMPTS

- major depression
- seasonal depression
- bipolar disorder
- anxiety disorder
- substance abuse
- conduct disorder
- oppositional defiant disorder
- impulse disorders
- attention-deficit/hyperactivity disorder
- schizophrenia
- post-traumatic stress disorder

GUNS AND SUICIDE

Accessibility to a gun greatly increases a teen's risk of completing suicide. A home with a handgun is almost ten times more likely to have a teen suicide than a home without a gun.

How many sixteen-year-olds fail their drivers' tests for fifteen years?

None. Absolutely none. And that's just the point. Suicide is a long-term fix for a short-term problem. It doesn't allow for the possibility of hope or change.

This short-term perspective, coupled with a teen's wanting immediate relief right here right now, mixed with depression and all of the other factors previously discussed, makes for a very dangerous formula. But these are only part of the suicide equation. Suicide is a complex issue, far bigger than can be adequately addressed here. It can't be reduced to simplified explanations, especially when in some cases, explanations won't be found.

Bullying, triggering circumstances, depression, and the rest only suggest suicide risk; they do not predict it. Again, as in all the other behaviors discussed in this book, suicide is a choice. And despite what a teen might feel at any given time, it is never the only choice.

How Do I Help a Suicidal Friend?

To help a friend see beyond suicide you first have to recognize whether or not that friend really is suicidal to begin with. Remember, everybody has "the blues" now and then: down days where they feel sad or discouraged. And it's perfectly normal to feel sad when a loved one or pet dies, or hurt when your boyfriend or girlfriend breaks up with you, or scared if you just found out you're pregnant. Sadness, discouragement, or even depression, doesn't necessarily lead to suicide.

A suicidal person may experience similar emotions, but he or she will also, in most cases, exhibit other warning signs:

- making statements of hopelessness and despair
- talking about death
- expressing the desire to die
- talking about or making a suicide plan
- losing interest in things that used to be important
- giving away personal possessions
- getting personal affairs in order, writing a will
- visiting or calling loved ones (even those not seen or talked to in a while)
- seeming suddenly happier or calmer after having been depressed
- suddenly doing extremely high-risk behaviors (unsafe sex, driving recklessly)
- saying goodbyes, or talking about "going away"

SUICIDE HOTLINES

To find a local suicide hotline in your area, visit the comprehensive directory of suicide hotlines listed by country and state (U.S., Canada, and international) online at

http://suicidehotlines.com.

OR

Call toll-free nationwide (U.S.): 1-800-SUICIDE (1-800-784-2433).

EARLY WARNING SIGNS OF SUICIDAL THINKING

- changes in eating or sleeping habits
- withdrawal from friends or family
- increased unexplained rebellious behavior
- running away
- increased or new drug or alcohol abuse
- drop in school performance
- personality change
- complaints of physical ailments that aren't real
- persistent boredom
- difficulty concentrating
- neglect of personal hygiene or physical appearance

(From the American Academy of Pediatrics.)

If you or a loved one experiences these warning signs, get help immediately. If you are with someone exhibiting these symptoms, do not leave him alone. Get help, even if your friend asks you not to. Call a coach, a religious leader, a teacher, a school counselor, a parent, or any other trusted adult. Or check in the front of your telephone book for a local suicide hotline. The U.S. National Suicide Hotline is 1-800-SUICIDE and can be reached toll-free from anywhere in the United States.

Let your friend know that you care and that you are willing to listen. Take his feelings seriously. Be willing to talk about death and suicide with him. Ask him if he has a plan, or if he's de-

Suicide & Self-Destructive Behaviors

cided when and where he will kill himself. If your friend lays out the plan for you, treat it as an emergency. Call 911 or the police or take the person to the nearest emergency room. Your taking him seriously just may save his life.

Adolescence Is a Risky Age

Attempted suicide is, of course, the most extreme risk-taking behavior a teen can take. But just being an adolescent comes with risk.

As we discussed in chapter 1, however, adolescence isn't about not taking any risks; it's about discovering which risks are healthy and worth taking. Moving into adulthood is, in some ways, all about taking risks. But no risk, no problem, no issue or thrill is worth dying or permanently injuring yourself for.

Choose today to take healthy risks. The thrill and high you'll experience with those will far outlast and out-thrill anything unhealthy risk-taking behaviors can offer.

Further Reading

Grollman, Earl A., and Max Malikow. *Living When a Young Friend Commits Suicide or Even Starts Talking About It*. Boston: Beacon Press, 1999.

Holmes, Ann. *Cutting the Pain Away*. Philadelphia: Chelsea House, 2000.

McGraw, Jay. *Life Strategies for Teens*. New York: Fireside, 2000.

Pledge, Deanna S. *When Something Feels Wrong: A Survival Guide About Abuse for Young People*. Minneapolis: Free Spirit, 2002.

Potash, Marlin S., Ed.D., and Laura Potash Fruitman. *Am I Weird or Am I Normal: Advice and Info to Get Teens in the Know*. New York: Fireside, 2001.

Simpson, Carolyn. *Understanding Compulsive Eating: A Teen Eating Disorder Prevention Book*. New York: Rosen Publishing Group, 2000.

Stewart, Gail. *Teens with Eating Disorders*. San Diego: Lucent Books, 2000.

Winkler, Kathleen. *Tattooing and Body Piercing: Understanding the Risks*. Berkeley Heights, N.J.: Enslow Publishers, 2002.

Packer, Alex J. *Highs!: Over 150 Ways to Feel Really, Really Good … without Alcohol or Other Drugs*. Minneapolis: Free Spirit Publishing, 2000.

Shandler, Sara. *Ophelia Speaks: Adolescent Girls Write about Their Search for Self.* Thorndike, Me.: Thorndike Press, 2000.

Young, Bettie B. *A Taste-Berry Teen's Guide to Setting and Achieving Goals: With Contributions by Teens for Teens.* Deerfield Beach, Fla.: Health Communications, 2002.

For More Information

If you need immediate help call the National Hopeline Network 1-800-SUICIDE (1-800-784-2433) to reach a certified crisis center twenty-four hours a day, seven days a week.

American Academy for Child and Adolescent Psychiatry
www.aacap.org

American Association of Suicidology
www.suicidology.org

The AWARE Foundation (Adolescent Wellness and Reproductive Education)
www.awarefoundation.org

National Association of Anorexia and Associated Disorders
www.anad.org

National Eating Disorders Association (NEDA)
www.NationalEatingDisorders.org

National Institute on Drug Abuse for Teens (NIDA)
www.teens.drugabuse.gov

National Mental Health Association
www.nmha.org

National Youth Violence Prevention Resource Center (NYVPRC)
www.safeyouth.org

Partnership for Drug Free America
www.drugfree.org

S.A.F.E. Alternatives (Self Abuse Finally Ends)
www.selfinjury.com

S.A.V.E (Suicide Awareness Voices of Education)
www.save.org

Check Yourself™
www.checkyourself.com

Something Fishy Website On Eating Disorders
www.something-fishy.org

Teen Central.Net
teencentral.net

Teen Resources On-line
www.teenresources.org

Teens 411
www.child.net/teenhelp.htm

TeensHealth Magazine
kidshealth.org/teen

Yellow Ribbon Suicide Prevention Program
www.yellowribbon.org

Youth Suicide Prevention website (Canada)
www.youthsuicide.ca

Publisher's note:
The websites listed on these pages were active at the time of publication. The publisher is not responsible for websites that have changed their addresses or discontinued operation since the date of publication. The publisher will review and update the websites upon each reprint.

Glossary

ANGST A feeling of anxiety, apprehension, or insecurity.

ANKH A cross having a loop for its upper vertical arm and serving, especially in ancient Egypt, as a symbol for life.

BIPOLAR DISORDER A psychological disorder characterized by the alternation between manic and depressive states.

BORDERLINE PERSONALITY DISORDER A condition characterized by impulsive actions, mood instability, and chaotic relationships.

BMX An abbreviation for bicycle motocross.

CARDIAC Of, relating to, situated near, or acting on the heart.

CARDIOVASCULAR SYSTEM The organs and tissues involved in circulating blood and lymph through the body.

CHRONIC Marked by long duration or frequent recurrence.

COGNITIVE BEHAVIORAL THERAPY Treatment that focuses on changing an individual's thoughts in order to change his or her behavior and emotional state.

DIURETIC A substance that tends to increase the flow of urine.

DOUBLE In bicycle motocross, a series of two jumps placed close enough together so a rider can make both with one action.

ENEMA The injection of liquid into the intestine by way of the anus.

GAP THE BANKS A bicycle motocross trick that involves jumping over the space between two sloped areas that are less than 90°.

HEPATITIS Inflammation of the liver.

HITCHING POST Part of a BMX course that looks like the hitching posts for horses used in the old west (a rounded railing across two posts about three-feet high).

HIV (human immunodeficiency virus) Any of a group of retroviruses that infect and destroy helper T cells of the immune system causing the marked reduction in their numbers that is diagnostic of AIDS.

INHIBITIONS Psychological restraints that discourage free or spontaneous activity.

JAUNDICE Yellowish pigmentation of the skin, tissues, and body fluids caused by deposits of bile pigments (bilirubin).

OBSESSIVE-COMPULSIVE DISORDER A type of anxiety disorder characterized by distressing, repetitive thoughts or impulses that are intense, frightening or absurd, followed by ritualized actions that are bizarre and irrational.

OSTRACIZED Excluded from a group by general consent of that group.

PANIC ATTACKS Sudden, intense feelings of fear and danger, accompanied by physical symptoms of anxiety, such as a pounding heart, sweating, and rapid breathing.

PSYCHOTIC Fundamental mental derangement characterized by defective or lost contact with reality.

RAPPELLING Descending by sliding down a rope passed under one thigh, across the body, and over the opposite shoulder or through a special friction device.

ROLL-INS Portions at the tops of BMX ramps that riders can use to roll into the ramp rather than dropping in over the vertical section of the ramp.

SCHIZOPHRENIA A psychotic disorder characterized by loss of contact with reality, accompanied by hallucinations, delusions, and disintegration of personality and conduct.

SEDATION The inducing of a relaxed easy state, especially by the use of drugs such as tranquilizers.

SPELUNKING The hobby or practice of exploring caves.

TABLETOP A bicycle motocross jump with a long, flat top. Some are as low as 2 or 3 feet. Others are as high as 6 feet.

TACTILE Of or relating to the sense of touch.

TICS Twitching motions of particular muscles, especially of the face.

TYPE II DIABETES A chronic disease that results when the body's insulin does not work effectively. Insulin is a hormone released by the pancreas in response to increased levels of sugar (glucose) in the blood.

Index

Picture Credits

Artville pp. 13, 90
Benjamin Stewart p. 74
Digital Vision pp. 101, 102
Elena Rostunova | Dreamstime.com: p. 104
EyeWire p. 86
iDream pp. 11, 72
Masterseries pp. 30, 52, 108
Photodisc pp. 21, 25, 39
Rick Lord | Dreamstime.com: p. 28
Stockbyte pp. 14, 35, 43, 50, 55, 62, 66, 93
Thinkstock pp. 56, 59, 64, 79

The individuals in these images are models, and the images are for illustrative purposes only.

Biographies

Joan Esherick is a full-time author, freelance writer, and professional speaker who lives outside of Philadelphia, Pennsylvania. Joan has contributed dozens of articles to national print periodicals, written spiritual and educational books, and speaks nationwide.

Mary Ann McDonnell, Ph.D., R.N., is the owner of South Shore Psychiatric Services, where she provides psychiatric services to children and adolescents. She has worked as a psychiatric nurse at Franciscan Hospital for Children and has been a clinical instructor for Northeastern University and Boston College advanced-practice nursing students. She was also the director of clinical trials in the pediatric psychopharmacology research unit at Massachusetts General Hospital. Her areas of expertise are bipolar disorder in children and adolescents, ADHD, and depression.

Dr. Sara Forman is a board certified physician in Adolescent Medicine. She has worked at Bentley Student Health Services since 1995 as a Senior Consulting Physician. Dr. Forman graduated from Barnard College and Harvard Medical School and completed her residency in Pediatrics at Children's Hospital of Philadelphia. After completing a fellowship in Adolescent Medicine at Children's Hospital Boston (CHB), she became an attending physician in that division. Dr. Forman's specialties include general adolescent health and eating disorders. She is the Director of the Outpatient Eating Disorders Program at Children's Hospital in Boston. In addition to seeing students at Bentley College, Dr. Forman sees primary care adolescent patients in the Adolescent Clinic at Children's and at The Germaine Lawrence School, a residential school for emotionally disturbed teenage girls.